WHEN
YOUR PARENT
REMARRIES
Late in Life

WHEN YOUR PARENT REMARRIES

Late in Life

MAKING PEACE WITH
YOUR ADULT STEPFAMILY

TERRI P. SMITH

with

JAMES M. HARPER, PH.D.

Adams Media
Avon, Massachusetts

Published by
Adams Media, an F+W Publications Company
57 Littlefield Street, Avon, MA 02322 U.S.A.
www.adamsmedia.com

ISBN 10: 1-59869-064-7
ISBN 13: 978-1-59869-064-4

Printed in the Canada.

J I H G F E D C B A

Library of Congress Cataloging-in-Publication Data
Smith, Terri P.
When your parent remarries late in life /
Terri P. Smith with James M. Harper.
p. cm.
ISBN-13: 978-1-59869-064-4 (pbk.)
ISBN-10: 1-59869-064-7 (pbk.)
1. Adult children—Psychology. 2. Remarriage—Psychological
aspects. 3. Parent and adult child. 4. Stepchildren.
5. Stepfamilies—Psychological aspects.
I. Harper, James M. II. Title.
HQ799.95.S55 2007
306.84—dc22   2007010859

This publication is designed to provide accurate and authoritative information with regard to the subject matter covered. It is sold with the understanding that the publisher is not engaged in rendering legal, accounting, or other professional advice. If legal advice or other expert assistance is required, the services of a competent professional person should be sought.

—From a *Declaration of Principles* jointly adopted by a Committee of the American Bar Association and a Committee of Publishers and Associations

Many of the designations used by manufacturers and sellers to distinguish their product are claimed as trademarks. Where those designations appear in this book and Adams Media was aware of a trademark claim, the designations have been printed with initial capital letters.

Material from "Laugh in the face of adversity: I'm not kidding" used with permission of the author, Dr. Barry Bittman.

This book is available at quantity discounts for bulk purchases.
For information, please call 1-800-289-0963.

Contents

CHAPTER 1 ❧ *"Why Is My Father Holding that Woman's Hand?"*

CHAPTER 2 ❧ *"What Is Your Intention with My Mother?"*

CHAPTER 3 ❧ *"What Do You Mean the Wedding Is in Two Weeks?"*

Foreword

Melanie sat in my therapy office, describing how she and her husband were fighting over how her siblings had treated her father when he remarried. Her dad had remarried only eighteen months after her mother died of cancer. She and her siblings were shocked and reacted by threatening to disown Dad if he went through with the wedding. He told them he was perfectly capable of making this decision; he was lonely, and they should mind their own business. He went ahead and got married, and they disowned him. Now five years later, she and all of her siblings continue to refuse contact with their father or his wife; they kept their children from the influence of their grandparent, and Melanie defended her siblings' actions in the face of her husband's criticism. While this is an all too common story in therapy, I shouted in my mind, "This need not be the case!"

When Terri Smith first approached me about being involved in writing *When Your Parent Remarries Late in Life*, I immediately thought of the case I described above. Numerous resources have been written for stepfamilies with young and adolescent children, but until now, there has been no resource to help adult children whose parent is remarrying. In my practice of thirty plus years as a marriage and family therapist, I have encountered numerous family members struggling to adjust to their stepfamily experience. I wish that this book had been written then because it is a resource that would help every stepfamily. I know we wrote it for adult children whose parent's remarriage is throwing them into a stepfamily, but many of the suggestions would help any stepfamily. This book is a must read for a parent of adult children who is considering remarriage, for the potential stepparent, and for the adult children who will, willingly or not, be faced with how to adjust to their parent's remarriage.

Writing the book has been fun, painful at times, but worth it. Terri's personal experience of having her father remarry and my professional experience of working with stepfamilies make a unique combination. Combine that with the stories of the many families who were interviewed for the book, and the result speaks to the heart of both parent and adult child. The flow of personal stories, the wisdom of clinical experience, and findings from empirical research mix nicely together to create numerous suggestions for dealing with such matters as how to cope with your parent dating, what to do about the wedding, what to call a new stepparent, how to keep loyalties to your deceased or divorced parent from sabotaging your relationship with your new stepparent. With people living longer, many who do not now think they will need this book will discover a need for it at some future time.

An interesting twist in the book is the creative use of Erik Erikson's eight stages of human development as a lens through which to view the transition of adult children as they adjust to different phases of their parent remarrying. While being an unusual application of Erikson's stages, it nonetheless helps validate feelings adult children typically have when their parent remarries. It does not stop there, however. Erikson's framework forms the basis of suggested actions that will help adult children successfully navigate each phase of their new transition in a stepfamily.

Parents who are considering remarrying will avoid several common mistakes if they will read this book. It will help them understand the perspectives of their adult children, communicate more openly, and face some of the challenges head on. Stepparents, likewise, will benefit from reading about anticipations, fears, and experiences of adult children in stepfamilies.

The remarriage of a parent presents new opportunities for growth, nurturing, and love. It does not have to negate any influence a deceased or divorced mother or father has had. It does require change and adjustment while holding out the possibility of adding new loving, supporting relationships. It is our hope that the many suggestions will help you navigate the path more smoothly and with greater passion and peace.

James M. Harper, Ph.D.

Acknowledgments

D r. Randy Bott challenged me to write a book on a subject I didn't understand. Thank you for giving me that challenge for it has changed my life for the better. My interviews and research increased my understanding of interpersonal relations and motivated me to make personal changes.

I am grateful to each individual and couple who shared their story with me of their parents' remarriage or of becoming a stepparent. Their experiences and insights are the core of this work. Their wisdom and examples helped me to improve my relationship with my father and stepmother.

I am thankful for the Robert G. Allen Institute for mentoring me in the process of getting my ideas and thoughts into print. The institute's coaches guided me in the procedure of writing and preparing a book proposal to present to publishing houses. They also answered my questions and gave feedback that helped me to prepare a successful book proposal.

After presenting my proposal to several editors whose companies publish books of my genre, Paula Munier of Adams Media believed in my ideas and offered me a contract. I appreciate her willingness to accept the work of a first-time author. Meredith O'Hayre worked closely with Ms. Munier in editing this work. Thank you. I also appreciate the efforts of my literary agent, Barbara Doyen, in working behind the scenes to negotiate the details of the contract. Her efforts allowed me to continue with my research and writing unencumbered by the additional research of the legalities of publishing contracts.

The editing and suggestions of friends and family, Susan Kimura, Sharon Jenni, Robert Potts, Debra McGill, Danielle

Freeze, Ed Darrell, and Bronwyn Llewellyn have been invaluable. They helped me to understand more clearly what I was trying to say and to focus on what is beneficial. I'm grateful to librarians Julene Butler, Marvin Wiggins, and Tom Wright of the Brigham Young University Harold B. Lee Library for their help with research.

Each individual offered an integral part in bringing this book to fruition. I am grateful to each one of them for their help as well as to my family and friends, who have encouraged me along the way. And a special thanks is extended to Dr. James Harper for his expertise as the technical reviewer.

My deepest appreciation is for the love, support, and sacrifices of my husband, Paul, and our children, Joshua, Allison, Jacob, and Benjamin. They willingly relinquished computer time while I wrote and rewrote. They assumed responsibility for meal preparation and other household chores. They provided encouraging words, a soft shoulder to cry on, and warm embraces throughout my research and the creation of this book. I love them dearly; they are precious to me.

Introduction

*"Understanding that rewarding relationships require effort
is a valuable insight at any age, providing new
opportunities for personal growth and enhancement
of existing relationships."*

—Dr. Sarah Corrie

If one of your parents has died, you have undoubtedly encountered the tumult of emotion that follows, from grief to sadness to remorse and everything in between. If your surviving parent has remarried within what seemed to you an uncomfortably short period after the funeral, all of the parties involved have probably experienced more than a few awkward moments, unsettling emotions, and surprising reactions. I felt all of these things, and more, after my mother passed away and my father remarried.

Logically, I knew that even the most joyous of life's experiences, such as birth, are attended by the shadow of pain and sacrifice. Marriage—the birth of a new family—is certainly a joyous event, but few would argue that a successful marriage demands effort, sacrifice, and, yes, pain. The setbacks and challenges of marriage are counterbalanced by love, companionship, and intimacy. Certainly all of life's most difficult passages—death of a loved one, divorce, remarriage—are full of opportunities for personal growth. Yet just knowing this doesn't help when you're in the throes of grief or anger. It didn't help me understand the negative emotions I was feeling. I wanted to be happy for my father and his new wife, but I also felt guilty and sad. I wanted to know why. I needed help, but I didn't know where to turn.

I found bookstores and Web sites full of resources for blended families with young or adolescent children, but not for me—a married adult with children of my own. Therapists and other experts stand ready to help children through what can be a difficult and even traumatic time. But what about the children who are no longer children? In an article published in the *Journal of Marriage and Family,* British psychologist Sarah Corrie wrote, "The characteristics and needs of adult children who are experiencing family reconfiguration have been largely ignored by both the research and clinical research." When a parent remarries, adult children face complicated adjustments, feelings, and divided loyalties. Adult children may experience anger at their biological parent and feel as though they must compete with the new partner for attention. Having a new stepparent often exaggerates grief over missing the deceased or absent parent. These feelings in turn lead to distress and confusion about what to do or where to turn. Adult stepchildren experience similar dilemmas and feelings as their adolescent counterparts when confronted with a new stepparent.

Yet adult children think that they're not "supposed to" feel upset or angry or excluded. After all, we're all adults here, right? I wanted someone to recognize how I felt—betrayed, confused, angry, lonely—with my mother gone and contact with my father diminished. You may be feeling the same way. You may struggle to mourn the loss while coping with your own family's day-to-day reality. You may feel robbed of the security of an old familiar family life. You may cling to memories, both happy and sad. You may be overwhelmed with regret to think of what you could have or should have done differently. Instinctively, you want to turn for comfort to someone you love and who loves you. If that person is no longer available because he or she has moved on with a new partner, a new life, and maybe a new family, it can turn your perception of how you fit in completely upside down. What I didn't realize was how many people shared my plight.

A Stepfamily Boom

Consider these figures: According to U.S. Census Bureau 2000 statistics, over 85 million Americans are over the age of 45; that group is now over 50. Government aging statistics for 2004 indicate that 44 percent of women and 21 percent of men over age 65 are widowed, divorced, or never married. In America, over 50 percent of first marriages and 60 percent of second marriages end in divorce, and older couples make up the fastest-growing group of divorcing people in the nation. Of those divorced people, three quarters will remarry. Writing for *Psychology Today* magazine, Hara Estroff Marano said, "…an estimated 500,000 people over the age of 65 remarry each year in the U.S., and many more between 45 and 64." According to psychologist Deborah Carr, only 2 percent of older widows and 20 percent of older widowers remarry. While this is not a substantial percentage, when you consider that these adults may have several children, a significant number of adults grapple with the realities of remarriage of one or both parents.

According to a 1992 article in *American Demographics*, approximately one in three Americans was a stepparent, stepchild, stepsibling, or some other member of a stepfamily. Just as astonishingly, according to the author, J. Larson, more than half of Americans have been, are now, or will eventually be in one or more step situations during their lives. It stands to reason that that number has increased in the last decade. That means there are tens of millions of people affected emotionally, spiritually, financially, and in many other ways by the stepfamily boom.

For the lucky ones, there is an instant bond among all parties involved. However, research suggests that the typical stepfamily relationship is a stressful one. Sometimes you don't accept or approve of your parent's choice of partner. Other times the new spouse doesn't like or accept you. Blending families is challenging when children are young; the remarriage of a parent can verge on disastrous when the children are adults. Communications could grow strained or stop completely. The family relationships you thought you could count on shift, and you could end up feeling even more adrift than ever.

Unfortunately, the stereotypical view of stepfamilies isn't pretty. The harmony of television's Brady Bunch family seems like the exception. What comes to mind when most people hear the words "stepmother" and "stepsisters" is the word "evil"! Overworked Cinderella was unfairly treated by her stepfamily. Snow White's stepmother wanted the poor girl killed. Hamlet's stepfather, also his uncle, murdered his father before marrying his mother, and pretty much everyone died by the end of that story. Be glad you aren't living in a Shakespearean tragedy—or a fairy tale.

In Search of a Training Manual

What I needed, I soon realized, was a "training manual" that would help me understand my new stepparent and work through this new family dynamic. Such was the impetus for my quest. I set out to meet and talk to as many people as I could who were members of mature stepfamilies. Some of their stepfamily relationships were strained, some broke completely, while others developed into cherished friendships. What made the difference? How did they cope? What did they think? How did they react? I hoped their insights would help me understand my own situation. I wanted to find behaviors and mindsets that could help others going through similar circumstances. What I discovered fills the chapters that follow.

Remarriage can bring a great deal of joy and happiness to the families involved. A willingness to labor and sacrifice for the benefit of the whole family goes a long way toward alleviating problems, but you can't force people to be generous of spirit. Selfishness, shortsightedness, and divided loyalties are just a few of the causes of stepfamily problems. It's human nature to circle the wagons and protect one's personal interests in the face of outsiders or apparent threats. We form opinions based on hearsay, rumor, or secondhand gossip. Some adult children even try to sabotage their parent's remarriage. Some succeed. Marriage is hard enough without family members actively working to derail it. It's no wonder more than 60 percent of second marriages end in divorce.

Lest you become too discouraged, know that there are many successful, mature stepfamilies. These individuals make loving relationships a priority and find ways to overcome the unavoidable challenges. They're rewarded with step-relationships that truly are abiding friendships.

You Have Options

For those of you in the midst of a parent's courtship or remarriage, my desire is to share some of the wisdom of those who have succeeded in nourishing healthy step-relationships. As you seek to understand and learn from your own experiences, you will discover value-based behaviors, such as honesty, kindness, and compassion, which can enhance your relationships and enrich your life. You can learn ways to replace the heartache and disappointment with peace and happiness. You, too, can be rewarded—with trust, security, love, and joy. That certainly sounds better than stewing in anger and resentment, doesn't it?

None of this will happen overnight, and it won't necessarily be easy. You'll have to accept responsibility for your behavior, thoughts, and actions. You'll need to learn how to distinguish between your emotions, over which you have little control, and your behaviors, which you can control. Perhaps most importantly, know that you have options. The scenarios that follow will help you see different perspectives and realize that you have alternatives beyond the first knee-jerk reaction.

These chapters are designed to help you follow the course of your parent's courtship, remarriage, and subsequent life, as well as your relationship to your parent and stepparent. Each chapter includes sidebars intended to help you see situations from your parent or stepparent's perspective, as well as the input of therapists and other experts. Also included in each chapter is a series of action steps that you can try in specific circumstances. Finally, each chapter concludes with some pointers, which I've called "The Heart of the Matter," for all of its ramifications— from core to compassion, essence to affection. I've included many examples taken from real life. The people I interviewed generously shared their experiences, both good and bad. My intention is not to judge them but to learn from them, as I hope you will do as well.

CHAPTER 1

"Why Is My Father Holding that Woman's Hand?"

"There are two primary choices in life: to accept conditions as they exist, or accept the responsibility for changing them."
—Denis Waitley

Unannounced, your widowed dad appears at your door with a female escort. Your dad rarely visits without an invitation, so right away, you know something is different. And who is this woman hanging onto his arm? Or your divorced mom excitedly tells you about a widower she met online. Two weeks later she invites you to join them for dinner at a local restaurant. They enter holding hands like a couple of teenagers. What is up with this? You knew dad was lonely, but he had told you he wouldn't marry after your mother died. Mom seemed content spending time with your family and volunteering at the hospital. Why are they now dating? Surely, they're not contemplating marriage, or are they?

One surprise at a time is all you can handle right now. Your main concern is this stranger who just entered your life and his or her intentions. If your mother is dating, chances are she shares everything with you about her male companions and their dates and keeps you informed as relationships progress. If your father is dating, you may not be aware of it for weeks. Perhaps a sibling, or worse yet, an acquaintance, informed you of your dad's activities. You're fortunate if you know your dad is dating. Some fathers surprise their children with a wedding invitation.

Why are they dating? In their research on "The Nature and Functions of Dating in Later Life," sociologists Richard and Kris Bulcroft report that in later life women generally date to find financial and status security, whereas men date to have someone to do things with and to hedge against loneliness. You can breathe a sigh of relief for the meantime. Though your parents are in the minority of their age group seeking companionship; nevertheless, they are dating. And you know that dating could lead to courtship and romance and eventually marriage, which is even a smaller minority. Your parent is looking for companionship and you have some influence over the outcome. Parents recognize some adult children resist a new marriage. Consider carefully your intentions as your parent re-enters the dating scene.

Dating indicates your parent's desire to move on in life. You may not be ready for your mom or dad to move on. You could deny your parent is dating, which only delays accepting the reality of it. You could ignore the dating and hope your parent loses interest, which usually doesn't happen. You could complain and protest, which may cause more harm than good and rarely changes a parent's mind. Or you could accept your parent's dating and reach out to new companions. Speaking from experience, the latter is the better choice.

Use the dating period to prepare for a possible marriage. As a son or daughter you are along for the ride, whether you like it or not. In some cases your opinion is irrelevant to parents, especially if they are already serious. You may not approve of their choice. However, whom they marry is, in fact, their choice. Parents are old enough to experience the consequences of their decisions whether good or bad. What can you do?

Accept the fact that your parent is dating. Just as you cannot change the fact the sun rises and sets each day, you cannot change your parent's behavior. Becoming acquainted with your mom or dad's companion is a wise choice—one may be your future stepparent. If you notice potential problems or red flags, acknowledge the warnings and discuss them with your parent. This is not meant to be blind acceptance. Keep in frequent contact. Acknowledge feelings of protectiveness. Watch out for that first public kiss or expression of affection. Romantic overtures may be uncomfortable for you, but they are a natural part of courtship.

Realizing Your Parent Is Dating

Once married, most people have no desire to return to the dating period of life. Dating is a guessing game. Does this person like me or is she just being nice to me? How long should I wait before calling? Yet, some parents who are once again single after the death of a spouse or a divorce find themselves desiring companionship in the later years of life. In her research on dating and remarriage of older widows and widowers, Dr. Deborah Carr found that "men are significantly more likely than women to want to remarry, to be interested in dating, and to be currently dating" six months after loss. At eighteen months after loss of a spouse, only 15 percent of adults reported interest in remarrying. Knowing that mom or dad is in the minority is of little comfort or value to you. Nor does it answer the myriad of questions circling in your mind such as: How can Dad date three months after Mom died? Why is Mom acting so silly suddenly? If my mom marries, what happens to our relationship? What will Dad do about money issues?

However, Dr. Carr's research does answer the question of what parents are seeking through dating: "Late-life romantic relationships may be sought as a source of emotional support and companionship rather than for instrumental support or economic stability. . . . The bereaved may be most interested in meaningful and supportive companionship." That is consistent with comments of adult children and couples I interviewed for my research. Dads expressed an overwhelming sense of loneliness and feelings of discomfort in social settings, even with family. Adult children noticed their mother's growing desire to date and remarry after eighteen months to two years after widowhood. Moms are more comfortable than dads in family activities, but they still return to an empty house that reminds them they are alone. Loneliness leads them to seek companionship. Dating offers that companionship and is preferable to being alone.

Dealing with Your Reactions

The dating period allows you time to mentally adjust to the reality of mom or dad having another partner and possibly remarrying. You, like some other children, may want to deny that your parent is dating or you may become angry that mom or dad is seeing someone. That is natural. It is strange thinking of mom or dad dating let alone remarried, but it becomes easier over time.

Denying your parent is dating only prolongs accepting reality. You may close your eyes to Dad's excuses to leave a family party early. Perhaps if you don't meet Mom's companion or hear about her dates, you won't have to deal with the possibility of marriage. Denying the fact your parent is dating may be a continuation of the grieving process. Eventually you have to accept reality with all of its ramifications, including marriage and modifications in relationships.

Though emotional reactions to your parent's social activities are normal, they may catch you off guard. For example, Laura's dad was widowed about a year when he began dating. "I'm an only child and had a close relationship with my parents. When my dad told me that he was dating, I was pissed. I couldn't believe he would date someone a year after my mom died. My reaction surprised me. I didn't think I would react like I did until it happened. Ten years have passed since my mother died, and my father hasn't remarried." Laura was concerned her verbal chastening of her dad may have adversely affected his social interactions.

Before reacting to initial emotions, consider the consequences. Negative behavior or unkind words often result in regret. Desiring your parent's happiness and best interest helps you focus on rationally discussing their dating and possible marriage. Spending time with your parent and asking questions may open your eyes to their loneliness and desire to move on. You may even enjoy the enthusiasm that has returned to Mom or Dad's life because of their repartnering.

The dating period allows you, the child, to adapt to another significant person in Mom or Dad's life. You hear the excitement in mom's voice as she tells you about her date to a play. You notice that Dad is more relaxed while visiting with his female companion. Comments about loneliness are no longer mentioned. They become less dependent upon you for social interaction.

Melanie was a single mom living at home when her widowed mother began dating. Melanie enjoyed watching her mother socialize and return home from activities for seniors with several marriage proposals. "I thought the proposals and my mom's beaux were funny. Oh, here's another one at the door. I enjoyed the dating phase for my mom and watching her go through the process. Then she and Dan met and married." Melanie loved her dad but had little interaction with him. When her mother dated Dan, who has a warm and welcoming personality, Melanie immediately felt accepted and easily reciprocated by inviting Dan into her life.

Initial Impressions Affect Acceptance

Not everyone has an easy transition with his or her parent dating. Sometimes, the problem could be an issue with the partner. Diane's mom began dating Jim, the husband of a deceased friend. "Jim and his wife never had a good relationship. My mom's friend complained about Jim to my mom. They separated before she was diagnosed with cancer and decided to remain married," Diane said. Jim had been married twice, so Diane had cause to be concerned when Jim started phoning her mom. "At first my mom was standoffish because of all the bad things she had heard of Jim." Diane's mom eventually accepted Jim's invitations for dates and they later married.

If you are aware of a potential stepparent's faults or problems, as Diane was, naturally you worry about your parent marrying the person. And your impression affects your interaction with and acceptance of him or her. You wait and watch for signs of this person's love and concern for your parent. Acceptance is withheld until clear evidence supports sincere commitment.

Contrary to Diane's experience, Scott had no preconceived notions of his new stepmother, Mary, which facilitated his acceptance of her. Mary described their initial encounter: "The first time I met Scott he said, 'Welcome to the family.' He threw his arms around me and called me mom from then on. Then Scott asked if he was going to have a sibling. That is Scott, and that really made me feel wonderful." Even though Mary was a few years beyond childbearing age, the comment eased any feelings of being uncomfortable. What a wonderful feeling to be accepted for who you are! Mary experienced that the first time she met Nick's children. It was unifying and she immediately felt accepted.

Dating partners come in a variety of personalities. The challenge is finding the right personalities that mesh together. As your parent explores potential companions while searching for another spouse, you may be adjusting to the thought of Mom or Dad with another partner. If you are having a hard time accepting your parent dating, acknowledge your feelings and label them, such as anger, jealousy, betrayal, etc. Separate the feelings from your desire for your parent's welfare. Wait until you are calm to discuss your concerns rationally with your parent. Recognize reassurances of your parent's love for you—for instance, mom's eagerness to share her activities with you—and your importance in Mom or Dad's life.

Life would be boring if everyone had the same personality traits. Mom's new companion may be the total opposite of her previous spouse. That is often the case. You may wonder what your parent sees in this person. Diane delineated the differences between her dad and stepfather: "Jim has a Ph.D., while my dad had a couple of years of college. Dad liked country music; Jim likes the opera and going to the ballet. My dad grew a vegetable garden and had cows, pigs, chickens, and horses; this guy grows dahlias. They are totally different in every way. It has been interesting to see how the differences in his personality have brought those things out in my mom, part of her personality we hadn't seen." As you accept your parent's dating, you, too, may notice how personalities blend, bringing forth latent interests.

Adjusting to the Idea of Mom or Dad Dating
Once you've accepted the fact that Mom or Dad is dating, the next step is getting used to the idea. Hearing about their dates,

7

seeing them together, and interacting with them may be awkward in the beginning, but as you continue to communicate and socialize, you become more comfortable with the idea of Mom or Dad having a new companion. Some parents, especially moms, keep their children informed of their activities. Others may tell you little or nothing of what they are doing. Open communication fosters trust and security. Little or no communication often results in hurt feelings and damaged relationships. Awareness of these differences may encourage you to interact with your parents and their dating companions during the courtship. Talking with your parents about their romances communicates your love for them and your interest in their lives. Likewise, your parents' sharing indicates your continued value to them. Withholding information from you may give the impression they are hiding something from you or make you feel like you are insignificant to them. Everyone desires to be loved and to feel a sense of belonging, especially when it comes to family. You may need to set the example by maintaining contact with Mom or Dad and even asking probing questions when necessary to know what is happening in his or her life.

The Importance of Communication

Parents should keep you informed of significant happenings and survey your reactions of potential partners. If or when they decided to marry, family support fosters marital success. In her book *Family Ties and Aging*, Ingrid Arnet Connidis explains, "Once married, older remarried couples tend to enjoy positive support from their children, who are happy because their parent is happy. This is fortunate because marital success is enhanced by positive feedback from family and friends." Interaction, observation, and communication are tools parents can use to measure your support or recognize your apprehension. Be honest and forthright during this period. You may feel that you need additional time to adjust to your parent dating, let alone the thought of marriage. Express your feelings, then remember that it is your parent's life and decision.

Desiring to stay close to their children, many single parents talk with their children regularly, sharing details of their lives. Talking to you during the courtship protects against surprise announcements. Women are more likely than men to talk with their children and communicate their fears, anxieties, and excitement about men they are dating and the possibility of another marriage. They want to share their feelings with someone they trust. You are the natural one for your mother to confide in since a new marriage will affect your relationship.

Steve's widowed mother, Shirley, called him frequently to let him know what was going on in her new relationship. She invited Steve and his wife along with his sister and her husband to dinner to meet Nolan, the man Shirley eventually married. They became acquainted and enjoyed being together. Steve saw and felt Nolan's commitment to his mother, and Nolan saw Steve's concern for her. Shirley's efforts to keep Steve informed helped him adjust to her dating and promoted acceptance of Nolan.

Some women may talk too much, as in Sandy's experience with her mother: "My mom told us pretty much everything. It was kind of funny. She's my mother. Some of the things I'd prefer not knowing, but she's very open."

Some men, particularly those in the golden-age generation, tend to be less communicative than women are about personal issues. They tend to keep their feelings and activities private. Dads answer your questions but are less apt than moms to volunteer information. Some men feel that it is their business what they do in their spare time. Regarding his dating, Trudie's dad told her, "It was something I wanted to do and enjoyed doing. I just didn't advertise it." Nick said, "My children knew I was taking a particular woman out. They could tell. I never mentioned her. I didn't think it was any of their business what I was doing. What I did was my business." Some dads don't realize when they marry, it affects the whole family. Throughout life men make decisions independently or in conjunction with their wife for the support or well-being of their family. Children are beneficiaries of their parents' decisions. Dad may not consider that as an adult, you might have an opinion or interest in his decisions. Some dads set themselves up for problems when they surprise their children with a wedding announcement and expect them to attend the ceremony and be jubilant. You may feel slighted because Dad has failed to inform you. Dads can learn much from their female counterparts regarding the importance of their interactions with their children and the consequences of little or no communication. Keeping you abreast of a developing relationship encourages you to be more receptive to their companion and marriage.

Mike's dad was quiet about what he was doing: "My mother died in October. In December one of my sisters told me that my dad was dating and had been for a month. That's how I found out. Dad told me in April of his engagement after some friends of mine told me he was getting married. So my dad really didn't let me know what he was doing." Naturally, Mike would have preferred hearing such news from his father rather than from a third party.

British psychologist Sarah Corrie observed feelings of rejection and loss of self-esteem among her adult stepchild clientele. These feelings may result when you learn of a parent's dating or pending marriage from an outsider rather than from your mom or dad. No wonder some children treat their parent's partner like an outsider. Love of family dictates that parents share with you at least a little bit about their developing romances.

Dr. John Gray describes this phenomenon in his book *Men Are from Mars, Women Are from Venus*: "When a Martian gets upset he never talks about what is bothering him. Instead he becomes very quiet and goes to his private cave to think about his problem, mulling it over to find a solution. When he has found a solution, he feels much better and comes out of his cave."

Loneliness is a problem confronting widowed men. Rather than discuss it, many men look for solutions—companionship. Once they have a new companion, the loneliness vanishes, the problem is solved, they come out of their cave, and they announce their wedding, sometimes to your surprise and chagrin.

On the other hand, women like to know what is happening and to share their feelings and experiences. Understanding these differences is especially helpful in father/daughter relationships. As a daughter you may sense that something is happening and question your dad until you obtain sufficient information to satisfy your interest and concern for him.

The following two examples portray this love and concern. Kristen recalled this interaction with her father: "We were at a family gathering and dad said, 'Well, gotta go.'

'Hey, dad, what are you doing?'

'Well, I have plans.'

'What kind of plans do you have?'

'Well, I'm going to a movie.'

'Who are you going with?'

'My brothers were going, *Shh. Shh.*' They were horrified that I would do that. I thought why not? I don't care if he's going to the movies with somebody. I wanted him to know that I care about him enough to know what he's doing and whom he's doing it with. It ended up being a friend that he played cards with." Kristen was fine with her dad dating; she wasn't upset or offended. She understands her father's personality and was willing to ask questions until she received sufficient information.

However, Trudie said she felt shut out by her father following a similar conversation. Trudie also wanted to let her dad know she loved him and wanted to be kept informed. She telephoned her father weekly after her mother's death. Soon thereafter Trudie said her father cut their conversations short. Trudie shared this interaction with her dad, "Well, I better go. I have things to do."

"What do you have to do, dad?"

"I have some visits to make."

"Who do you have to visit, dad?"

"Oh, people."

"Who, dad?"

"Helen Johnson."

Not understanding the general nature of men, Trudie felt like her father was trying to hide his developing romance and exclude her from his life; and consequently, she felt a growing distance between them. Trudie would have been fine with her dad dating had he been open about it. Once Trudie's dad had a solution to his loneliness, he came out of his cave, announced his wedding in two weeks, and expected everyone to rejoice with him. Trudie said her dad was completely unaware her feelings were hurt. As Trudie experienced, any perception of deceit (real or imagined) causes offense and destroys trust. Even if you feel that your parents are not honest with you, be honest with them.

Richard is an only child and lives in a different state than his dad, George. Richard's father was widowed a couple of years before he began dating a widowed acquaintance. George kept his relationship quiet until just before the wedding. Richard was surprised by a phone call from his dad: "About two weeks before the wedding date, dad called and told me he was getting married. The date had been set much earlier but my dad had been reluctant to say anything about it. I think he was afraid of what my reaction would be." Richard was happy for his father, but he was unprepared for the wedding announcement since he was unaware his father had been seeing anyone. Getting used to the idea of your mom or dad with another partner is difficult when you are not informed your parent is dating.

Knowing what family members are doing represents a natural care and concern for those you love. You value being informed of your parent's romantic interests. You know these budding relationships could ultimately affect your family unit. Your parent's open discussion of his or her activities is preferable to learning of them from a third party. Being kept in the loop fosters fulfilling relationships and helps you adjust to changes.

Positive behaviors and forthright communication between you and your parent during dating and courtship form the foundation of loving, healthy relationships. You feel like a vital part of your parent's life. Open and regular communication between you and a potential stepparent also helps to prevent misunderstandings in the emerging relationship, and it encourages further interaction in the event of marriage. These honest interactions help you to weather difficulties as they arise, reduce future problems, promote unity, and help maintain trust and confidence, which most parents try to instill in their children.

Getting Acquainted

Courtship is that magical time of romantic relationships when couples discuss their hopes and dreams. They learn of each other's likes and dislikes and try to determine if they want to spend the rest of their lives together. They introduce potential mates to family members to see how well they get along. Introductions to adult children are a bit different from introductions to parents. Nevertheless, courtship is an ideal time for your parent to create opportunities for you to become acquainted with a potential fiancé(e). Since it may be the beginning of a long-term relationship, accept social invitations and put forth the effort to know this person. Extend a hand of friendship and invitations of your own to interact socially. During a dinner together or a game of tennis doubles you can learn much about a potential stepparent's mannerisms and personality. You may have foreboding premonitions to consider. This stranger may be sizing you up as well.

Warm and welcoming behavior offers acceptance that others tend to reciprocate. Ruth summed it up concisely: "I think that when we accept people, then they will accept us." Relationships may not always be that simple, but that is a great way to start. Keep an open mind throughout the courtship by giving this potential stepparent the benefit of the doubt.

A Child's Perspective

Many prey upon the elderly by seeking financial assets whether modest or substantial. Could Mom or Dad's dating partner be one of those preying? That is a possibility. But perhaps he or she truly loves your parent and has no hidden agenda. Be cautious in what you say and do, for it may come back to haunt you.

Take advantage of opportunities to interact with a future stepparent during the courtship. Begin by learning of each other's interests, concerns, personality traits, etc. Be yourself (unless you don't like some of your behaviors, in which case this is your chance to change) and be honest in your interactions, which increases the likelihood of accepting each other, especially if you are a good person. Spending time together enables you and your parent's future spouse to ease into a new relationship. You also witness the joy of your parent with another companion.

Sandy's mother was widowed with five children; her stepfather, Dean, was widowed with nine children. Sandy said, "Before they married, we had dinners together and one big family dinner so everyone could meet, so we knew Dean and his family. My mom met Dean's children and had a good rapport with them. All but one daughter fell in love with my mom like we fell in love with Dean." Speaking of Dean, Sandy commented, "He has been exceptional, a really neat husband and stepdad."

Sandy's close proximity to her mother, Elaine, enabled her to interact with her mom and Dean during their courtship. She observed how Dean treated her mother and saw a new sparkle in her mother's eyes. Elaine and Dean orchestrated opportunities to meet each other's children and for them to meet each other—a sign of the importance of their families and a good indicator that they would initiate further family interaction.

Kristen's dad was widowed with nine children. Her stepmother, Mary, was widowed with four children. Kristen's father lived in a different state when he began dating Mary. Kristen said, "I called my dad frequently to check on him. Dad isn't much of a communicator and has a hearing problem. After he started dating Mary, he quickly passed the phone to her and said, 'Here, talk to Mary.' I found myself talking with a stranger. I thought it was odd, but we eventually became acquainted through our phone conversations." Initially uncomfortable speaking with a stranger, Kristen made the effort to converse with Mary and gradually felt more at ease talking with her. When they finally met in person, Kristen and Mary felt like they were renewing an old friendship.

In the above examples, everyone involved made efforts to get acquainted and learned to trust each other. Kristen and Mary developed a cherished friendship. Sandy experienced a parental support from Dean that she lacked from her father. Dinners, parties, phone calls, and other activities provide opportunities for families to get acquainted. You may notice the care and tenderness given to your parent. You appreciate the interest a future stepparent expresses in you and your family. Social events and kind behavior throughout the courtship encourages mutual acceptance and trust.

A **Stepparent's** Perspective

During his courtship with Ruth, Dave, a widower with no children, spent a lot of time with Ruth's family. Ruth was widowed with five children. Ruth invited Dave to all of her family get-togethers—birthdays, holidays, and other events. Ruth's children saw Dave's love for their mother and Dave and Ruth's pleasure in being together. The children felt Dave's interest in them as he asked them questions and interacted with them and their children. They grew to love him, and he loved them.

On the other hand, the lack of social activities and interaction can result in parental distrust and skepticism of a future step-parent. For example, Mike invited his dad to his daughter's birthday party, and he agreed to come: "We knew my dad was dating someone. On the same evening, he also planned to attend an activity with this woman he was seeing. A bad snow-storm that night prevented him from attending either event. I remember being hurt by my dad's failure to come and feeling bad for my daughter. I felt that my family and I were no longer important to him. So I didn't make any effort for some time to further the relationship. I felt like it was my dad's life and he would do what he wanted to do." Mike lost confidence in his father's emotional support, forming a rift in their relationship that broadened when Mike ceased trying.

Mike's relationship with his dad illustrates why some mature stepfamilies struggle. Mike's sisters informed him his dad was dating. He felt little effort on his dad's part to communicate with him, to keep commitments, or to initiate social interaction with the woman whom he eventually married. Consequently, Mike stopped making an effort. Eventually, he extended invitations to his dad and stepmother. However, once trust and confidence are tarnished, time and effort must be invested to

16

restore them. Relationships can't progress or even begin without mutual effort.

Rather than being a hindrance to your parent's blossoming romance by treating Mom or Dad's companion as an outsider, get to know this person and extend a hand of friendship. Rather than offering resistance, have an open mind. They just might fall in love. If you've established a good rapport, you have a foundation to continue your relationship. Making the effort to get acquainted and to understand each other builds trust, may ease tension, and may prevent possible resentment—paving the way for acceptance.

Take Action

You suspect your parent is dating, but he or she has said nothing to you. Being concerned for Mom or Dad's welfare, you could be direct and ask if he or she is seeing anyone special. A direct question requiring a yes or no response puts your parent on the spot while allowing her or him the opportunity to share with you.

Keep in touch with your parents, and invite them to family activities. Query Mom or Dad about her or his welfare and activities. Be open-minded if your mom or dad mentions she or he has begun socializing.

You could ignore signs of dating and wait for your parent to broach the subject, but be advised that this option may catch you off guard with a surprise wedding invitation.

Possible Scenario

During the past few weeks your dad's behavior changed. Perhaps he met a new acquaintance and she is monopolizing his time, yet he hasn't mentioned it. Here is a suggestion for how to obtain information.

Child: (telephoning dad) Hi, dad. I tried to call you several times last night and no one answered.

Parent: I was out for the evening.

Child: I figured that. After a couple of hours, I began to worry since you are usually home in the evening. What were you doing?

Parent: I had an appointment.

Child: What kind of appointment did you have at night?

Parent: I met someone walking on the track, and we decided to have dinner together.

Child: You mean you had a date? You haven't been in the dating scene for many years. Well, fill me in. What's her name? What is she like? Are you planning to see her again?

Parent: What is this—twenty questions?

Child: I just want you to know that I love you, and I'm concerned about your welfare.

The Heart of the Matter

Successful stepfamilies do not begin at the altar; rather, the foundation is laid during the courtship. Dating is a time of acceptance—of the reality of this phase in your parent's life, of social interactions, and of one another. Put forth the effort and value the endeavors of your parent and his or her partner to become acquainted during the dating and courtship period.

➤ Dating is sometimes awkward for parents, but it is preferable to being alone. It indicates they are ready to move on in their lives following divorce or death of a spouse.

➤ Communication during the dating stage helps you get used to the idea of your parent dating. It also fosters trust and security, both desirable elements of successful relationships. Keep in touch with your parent by calling and visiting frequently, which provides opportunities for them to share their activities with you. Efforts to keep in touch and be informed represent your love and concern for parents and let them know they are an integral part of your life. Reassure your parents that you are okay with them dating and are simply interested in how these relationships are going.

➤ Use courtship as a time to become acquainted with your parent's future spouse. Accept and initiate social invitations to get to know each other. Plan a dinner or other activity. If you are married with children, single, or live a distance from your parent, give special consideration to get to know your parent's fiancé(e) and to develop your desired relationship. If you accept your parents' companions for who they are and what they add to your family, chances are they will accept you.

CHAPTER 2

"What Is Your Intention with My Mother?"

"One must never lose time in vainly regretting the past or in complaining against the changes which cause us discomfort for change is the essence of life."
—*Anatole France*

Seeing Mom or Dad with a new companion or hearing about their latest date has been a bit of an adjustment. You may feel like you've adapted well to these changes. However, upon meeting some dating partners, your initial impression is discomforting. What is the best course of action? Your options include waiting to see if the relationship progresses or fizzles on its own, sharing your feelings with your parent, or confronting your potential stepparent. You are the best judge, as you are acquainted with the players and the situation.

Red Flags

Deep inside you have your parent's best interest at heart. You've accepted the reality of Mom or Dad dating; you've even done a few things together socially. Intuitively, something doesn't feel quite right. A foreboding feeling gnaws at your heart, a feeling different from simply suspecting ulterior motives. Accepting Mom's or Dad's dating does not mean you close your eyes to warning signs of potential problems. You may notice signs of trouble such as controlling behavior, presenting an ultimatum, jealousy, drastic change in personality (be careful with this one since many people have a personality change when they begin dating), restricting contact with family, blaming others for problems or feelings, verbal abuse, constantly checking up on a partner, multiple marriages, as well as others. Recognize red flags as signs of potential danger and discuss them with your parent.

Once cautionary advice is given, respect your parent's decisions. Parents are usually quick to protect children, even adult children, from danger, potential mistakes, or inappropriate behavior. How you react to the warning is your choice, and you reap the consequences. The same is true for your parents. A warning may not change their behavior or decision, but at least you voiced your feeling.

Diane and her siblings worried when their mother discussed dates with Jim. Aware of his second wife's complaints about him, Diane and her siblings discussed their concerns with their mother. Diane even confronted Jim: "I was forthright with my stepdad from the beginning. When they were dating, Mom had Jim over to dinner one night and he was being all cozy with her. I said, 'What are your intentions with my mother? I need to know. I have a vested interest. What's going on here?'

'Well, I really like her and I like to spend time with her.'

'Do you love her? Are you planning to marry her? What's going on?'

'Well, I don't know. We haven't gotten that far. Maybe some day I would like to.'

'Let me express some concerns to you. My mother is a good woman and she has a tender heart.' My mom was sitting there dying. I said, 'But you've been married twice before, which tells me that you have a track record going here and I don't know what the problem is. I know it takes two people to have problems, but she was married once, happily for forty years. So I don't want to see her getting into something that is going to hurt her. I'm worried about that.'

'Oh, I would never hurt her. I will always treat your mother well.'

'I really hope so, because she has seven children who would hurt you if you hurt her.'" Nevertheless, Diane's mom and Jim married. Diane's family has experienced some challenges throughout the marriage.

You do have a vested interest in your parent's welfare and will do as much as you can to protect Mom or Dad. You want them to be happy. Parents are vulnerable because they are lonely, and you feel a responsibility to protect them, especially mothers. You don't want anyone taking advantage of Mom or Dad. Some children express their concerns to their parent, while others, like Diane, interrogate the perspective spouse. These reactions are normal and let parents know that you love them and are watching out for them. The dating partner also becomes aware of your protectiveness.

If the potential partner's motives are pure, he or she will not be offended, but rather will appreciate your concern for your parent's welfare. Such was the case with Nick. He wasn't offended when Mary's daughter questioned him: "The second time I met Mary's daughter, she asked, 'Just what are your intentions?' She was dead serious." Nick chuckled as he related this incident. As a senior citizen, his motives were scrutinized. Though he barely knew Mary's daughter, he felt her love and concern for her mother.

A **Parent's** Perspective

A few days before Christmas, Pam and her husband-to-be invited all of their children to a party to announce their wedding plans. At the conclusion of the evening, Pam hugged each child as they said goodbye. "One son whispered in my ear, 'Mom, are you settling?' 'No, I'm not settling.' I had that gut feeling for two weeks that what he said was true. Your kids have a lot of intuition. They know you and what kind of person would be good for you. I knew his warning came out of love and concern for me, but he respected my right to make a decision." Pam went through with the wedding. Though it wasn't an abusive marriage, it was not a happy marriage and ended in divorce.

In some instances, your parent may recognize potential problems and end a relationship without you having to say anything. For example, Steve was concerned when his mother dated someone who seemed to have a domineering personality. Steve was relieved when they stopped dating. Yet he was pleased when his mom met Nolan, whom she married: "I was protective but at the same time I was anxious because Mom needed a lot of attention. Mom went with us on all our family vacations from the time that my dad died until she remarried. She was at our house a lot supporting our kids, but not happy either. So I was glad for her marriage and for someone to fill that gap." Steve wanted his mother to remarry and was sensitive to the personalities of the men she dated. He was unwilling to sacrifice her happiness simply for companionship.

With your parent acting like a teenager rather than a senior citizen, you may at times feel more like a guardian than a child, watching out for your parent's welfare. You want to protect Mom or Dad as much as possible from unnecessary pain. Parents don't need additional pain, especially after the death of a spouse, a divorce, or years of being single. They deserve joy and happiness throughout the latter years of their lives. You want your parents to be happy, yet you fear that someone might try to take advantage of them. Be sensitive to your intuition and offer counsel when appropriate.

Some red flags may not be noticeable during the dating period. For instance, Cara's marriage ended in divorce after nineteen years. She dated for a couple of years, then one relationship became more serious. Brad was kind and thoughtful. He attended all of Cara's family activities. He was considerate and attentive to Cara and her family. Cara's children supported and encouraged the relationship. Brad never invited Cara to activities with his children. "That should have been a red flag," Cara said. Cara met Brad's children after she and Brad were married: "Brad's children are wonderful people, but perhaps they would have warned me about their dad." Soon after their wedding, his deceitful behavior became apparent and led to the disintegration of their marriage. Dishonesty of any type is a warning sign of potential problems, and when discovered, problems may be irreconcilable.

Trust, achieved through honest interactions, is essential for successful relationships. Integrity gives you a confident expectation that you can rely upon your parents and they can depend upon you through life's experiences. Honesty of a potential stepparent eases your concerns of ulterior motives of the marriage. If deceit is perceived, be honest with yourself by acknowledging feelings of warning. Share your concerns with your parent rather than regretting problems after they arise.

Romance

Perhaps you can't recall the last time you saw your parents being affectionate in front of you when they were still a couple. Things are different with this new companion. They are constantly holding hands and sitting close together. You may wonder why they are acting strangely or who is inhabiting your parent's body. Love is the reason behind the changes. Sociologists Richard and Kris Bulcroft report, "Research suggests that interest and capacity for sexual relationships continues in old age. In addition, the overall need for intimacy remains in the later stages of life."

The physical relationship of a mature couple in love is similar to young couples in love. They like holding hands and touching each other. It's a natural desire and part of the developing relationship. You may find it awkward and uncomfortable at times, but rest assured that the excitement of new love diminishes, and along with that there is less public display. In the meantime be happy that your parents still have live wires that create romantic sparks.

Melanie was caught off guard the first time she saw Dan kiss her mother: "I remember the first time I saw Dan come up behind my mom in the kitchen and put his arms around her and kiss her. I thought, *Ooooooh, my goodness! My mother just got kissed!* That was kind of weird in the beginning. But I have come to appreciate it as one of the ways Dan shows his love for my mother." Although that first kiss was a surprise, Melanie adjusted to it.

Most adult children are uncomfortable with romantic overtures between their mom or dad and someone other than their parent. Dr. Corrie describes it as "disliking overt signs of a parent's sexuality (such as witnessing the new couple hold hands, embrace or flirt)." Sarah said, "What was really weird for me was my parents' physical relationship with their partners. They were all lovey-dovey and demonstrative, which was uncomfortable for me."

That uncomfortable feeling may continue after the wedding. Diane's mom and Jim bought a new house after they married, and Diane's family moved in with them while job hunting.

Diane described her reaction to romantic overtures: "Mom and Jim had been in their house for a couple of months. Living with them for two months was the worst two months of my life. We would be talking, then Jim would give my mom an eye look, something that meant *I need some action*. Mom would say, 'Well we're going to bed now.' Okay, it's six o'clock. Good night. That was a little strange, as was seeing Mom holding Jim's hand."

Your parents' thirty, forty, or fifty-year marriage covers your entire life. Though they still loved each other as you were growing up, their public display of affection probably wore off long before you could remember it. You are comfortable with how Mom and Dad interacted. You don't know anything different. It is hard to imagine, or even worse, to see Mom or Dad being affectionate with anyone else. You may experience feelings of regret or sorrow if you did not hear or see affection expressed between your parents.

For example, Trudie said, "I had never heard my parents express or show love to each other. So it was hurtful for me to hear my dad and Helen express love to each other. They were visiting at my home when I heard Helen say, 'I love you.' 'I love you, too,' came my dad's response. It caused me to wonder about my parents' relationship and why my dad's behavior had changed."

It was odd for Sandy to see the physical interaction between her mom and stepfather, Dean: "It drove me nuts, and not because it was Mom and Dean, but because they were old and they acted like teenagers. They were all over each other. They sat right beside each other. It was funny because my mom had a friend who married soon after my mom and Dean did, and my mom said, 'They're so sickening.' We laughed. Like Mom wasn't. It seemed strange for them to be so giddy. I've learned since then that is normal. It was odd until they stopped acting like that."

New love at any age even with "old" parents causes romantic sparks. They like being together, sitting close to each other, and holding hands. It is natural when two people are in love, even if they are your parents.

Seeing his mom and Nolan show affection to each other was awkward for Steve at the beginning of their relationship, then the newness of love wore off and the public display of affection subsided: "It is common for a newlywed couple to be more affectionate than a long-married couple in almost all situations. Even though the long-time relationship may be good and strong, there's less of that public display of affection that newlyweds have. It's weird to see your parent at age sixty holding hands and touching a new spouse. For a while I ignored it because it wasn't that comfortable, but with time I got used to it. I imagine that it is a fairly common experience for children."

Romance truly does blossom at any old time or age. Romantic overtures are a natural part of relationships. Mature newlyweds enjoy being together, touching each other, and expressing affection just as much as young couples do. Learn to ignore it, accept it, or appreciate it until it wanes or becomes natural for you to see.

Be Flexible

If you have children of your own, you have watched your children grow, learn, mature, and accept more and more responsibility. It's fun to watch them develop; yet every stage of parenting has its challenges and anxiety. You learned how to adjust to each phase of childhood and adolescence—even those phases you thought were impossible or would never end. The ability to adapt helps you remain calm and enjoy your kids. The same holds true in your relationship with your parent and stepparent, which also has its various phases, albeit not as well defined or sequential as those in childhood.

Consider the eight stages of social-emotional development presented by psychiatrist Erik Erikson in 1956 and how they fit into your relationship with a potential stepparent. While this is a new application of Erikson's stages, it might help in understanding the development of your new relationship.

The first stage of trust versus mistrust usually occurs during the dating period as you wonder about ulterior motives. Your parent's behavior may also raise questions, casting doubt on the trust you placed in Mom or Dad if they are not forthright about developing relationships or act in ways contrary to their teachings and values.

The second stage of learning autonomy versus shame manifests itself by exercising your independence, sometimes through stubbornness or negativism. You may not agree with your parent's decisions and try to persuade them to accept your way of thinking.

The third stage is learning initiative versus guilt, or in other words, learning new skills, cooperating, leading as well as following, or becoming fearful and dependent upon others. You can allow your reservations about your parent's marriage to consume you, or you can give your stepparent the benefit of the doubt and initiate interaction.

The fourth stage is industry versus inferiority, which is indicative of your competence of developing new relationships. You learn to relate to Mom or Dad and your stepparent according to new roles and master appropriate social skills promoting unity. On the other hand, inferiority is a defeatist attitude leading to failure, inability, or unwillingness to have a relationship.

The fifth stage, learning identity versus role confusion, fits in well with the topic of new and old roles. Who am I? How do I fit into this new union?

The sixth stage is learning intimacy (love) versus isolation. Your choice is to isolate yourself from your parent or to open your heart with love to embrace your stepparent.

The seventh stage is generativity (sense of accomplishment) versus stagnation (self-absorption). How much do you care about others in working productively and creatively to redefine your new family structure?

The final stage is integrity versus despair. According to Childdevelopment.com, "The mature adult develops the peak of adjustment; integrity. He trusts, he is independent and dares the new. He works hard, has found a well-defined role in life, and has developed a self-concept with which he is happy. He can be intimate without strain, guilt, regret, or lack of realism, and he is proud of what he creates." If any social or emotional conflicts in the first seven stages are unresolved, you may experience despair in your present situation.

Your ability to face changes, resolve emotional conflicts, and stay flexible will enhance your capacity to remain calm and to think clearly through the inevitable miscommunications and troubles. As an adult, you have passed through most of these eight stages at least once throughout your life, gaining experience along the way. You are aware of your social strengths and weaknesses. Use your strengths to learn and progress through each phase of your relationship development. Strive to overcome weaknesses by turning them into strengths. A healthy adaptation in each stage leads to integrity—"the peak of adjustment"—a much pleasanter outcome than despair. The former leads to healthy, happy relationships, while the latter deteriorates them. Regardless of how your parent or stepparent behaves, your good and kind choices in handling most situations bring peace of mind. Learn from failures and mistakes along the way to avoid repeating them and to guide future choices. Flexibility and successfully progressing through each stage affects your happiness.

Your challenge, then, is to adapt to the changes in your family reconfiguration. A rigid attitude will more likely increase your anxiety and, ultimately, harm—even sever—your relationship with your parent and stepparent. Family life professor Jason S. Carroll, writing in *BYU Magazine*, notes, "Marriages [stepfamilies for our discussion] that recognize that relationships take work, . . . and that all relationships have differences that can be handled constructively—are better equipped to adapt to whatever joys and challenges may come."

Both of your parents shaped and molded you. Whether death or divorce separated them, their example and teachings continue to influence your life. As an adult, you don't want a replacement for either one; however, you can never have too many friends who love and care for you. Consider this potential marriage as an opportunity to make a new friend. Your relationship may evolve to the point that you feel very close to your stepparent, maybe even closer than you felt to your deceased parent. But that takes time.

This is an opportunity to build a new, supportive relationship, not one that replaces your relationship with your deceased parent, but a new relationship with new and interesting dynamics.

Trust Versus Mistrust

Erikson placed trust versus mistrust as the first stage of development occurring during infancy. This stage influences the rest of the baby's life. A well-nurtured and loved baby learns to trust his or her caregiver and feels secure, which leads to basic optimism. A baby who is handled poorly becomes insecure and mistrustful and possibly pessimistic. Compare this description with the infancy period of your relationship with a potential stepparent and with your parent during their courtship. A parent who keeps his or her children informed of courtships and marriage plans nurtures their relationship. Communication is open and mature, inspiring trust. Adult children maintain a sense of security knowing that they are valued confidantes. The reserved parent who keeps romances private builds a barrier between him or her and their children, giving the impression that their children cannot be trusted to support their activities. Mistrust breeds mistrust, leading children to wonder if they can rely upon their parent to foster family loyalties. As for the stepparent, adult children are at times naturally suspect of the new partner's motives and intentions. Lack of interaction may perpetuate suspicions, casting doubt on the quality of relationships after the wedding. Just as a baby's life is impacted by his ability to trust, your relationship with Mom or Dad and your stepparent is influenced by the conditions of this early period of learning to trust or mistrust.

Marriage and family therapists suggest that this period of trust building described previously is one of the most important steps in establishing a secure bond. Spending some positive time with both your parent and your new stepparent—but not too much and not too little—will help you form an attachment to them. They can help you build trust by stating explicitly that you will always have a place with them.

Take Action

What is the best strategy for handling feelings of suspicion as in Diane's situation? Given the fact that Jim's first marriage ended in divorce and his second wife complained about him, Diane's suspicions were justified; however, not all suspicions are justified. The first order of business is to examine your concerns and determine if they are founded on reasonable grounds or if they are selfishly motivated.

If your concerns are sound, you could discuss them with another family member or family friend for confirmation and support. Rationally discuss your concerns with your parent. You could even confront Mom or Dad's partner as Diane did.

If you are uncomfortable with face-to-face confrontations, an alternative is to write your concerns and send them to your parent.

You could adopt a wait-and-see attitude. The relationship may fizzle on its own, along with your concerns. If the relationship continues and your concerns increase, you can confront your parent at that time.

If your concerns are selfishly motivated, then the problem lies within you. You could spend more time getting acquainted. Consider Mom or Dad's needs and the consequences of a possible marriage and of your parent remaining single. You could discuss your attitude and resistance with a trusted family member, friend, or professional.

Possible Scenario

Having met Mom's fiancé something inside you whispers, "Something isn't quite right?" You've tried to brush it off, but the feeling persists. Now is the time to share it with your mom.

Child: Mom, ever since I met your fiancé, I've had an unsettling feeling that something is wrong.

Parent: Perhaps you're just nervous about it happening so quickly.

Child: You may be right. But how well do you know him? What do you know about him?

Parent: I know that I enjoy being with him. I know he loves me and I love him. I know that he's retired and likes to travel and so do I.

Child: That description doesn't tell me much about his character or personality. Mom, please just take some time to learn more about him and find out what he is really like. I love you and don't want unpleasant surprises after the wedding.

The Heart of the Matter

Flexibility is one of the characteristics of successful relationships. Accepting romantic overtures as natural signs of intimate relationships and building relationships founded on trust will help you adjust to changes in your family configuration.

- Red flags provide a warning of potential problems. Warning signs are exactly that—a warning. Avoid regret by recognizing red flags and foreboding feelings and discussing concerns with your parent. Be careful not to accuse or blame your parent when you express your concerns. After you've expressed your concerns, it is still your parent's decision; be willing to accept it. If you confront a potential spouse, be bold in gathering information while making apparent your concern for Mom or Dad.
- Seeing your parent be affectionate or hearing expressions of love to a new companion may be awkward. Physical attraction and romantic overtures are natural for engaged and newlywed couples, even at your parent's age. Accept and appreciate it until you are comfortable with it or until

it tapers off. Be happy your parent has someone to enjoy this facet of life with rather than being lonely.

- Accept your parent's dating partners for who they are without trying to change them. Look for the best in them and focus on their good qualities. Be gracious toward them, because one may become your stepparent. Accepting your parent's decisions and companion prepares you to rejoice with them on their wedding day and to make their marriage a success.

CHAPTER 3

"What Do You Mean the Wedding Is in Two Weeks?"

"When stepfamilies succeed in creating a nurturing life together, as many ultimately do, it is a striking human achievement."
— *William J. Doherty*

You've accustomed yourself to the idea of your widowed mom or divorced dad going out on a few dates. There's no harm in your parent having some fun. You imagine some dinners out, tennis, maybe a movie every now and then with various friends. You would be perfectly content if things went on just like this. Then you get the wedding invitation.

If your parent is not naturally communicative, this can come like a bolt out of the blue. Perhaps your stepparent-to-be has barely said ten words to you until now—or you have yet to even meet him or her. You may have been excluded from any preparations and only hear about the wedding weeks or days before the event. Maybe your prospective stepsiblings—but not you—have all been included in the wedding party. There's a good chance that you feel as though a complete stranger is

37

about to become a rather permanent fixture in your life. And you're supposed to rejoice?

In reality, your parent's remarriage shouldn't come as a complete surprise. Nearly three-quarters of the people whose first marriages end in divorce get remarried—why not your parent? And look on the bright side: they could have eloped. If you've been invited, your mom or dad is undoubtedly anxious for the whole family to celebrate the new marriage. It's just that sometimes that can be tough.

Some of the adult children I interviewed felt emotionally distressed by a parent's decision to remarry. This is a normal reaction that generally goes away as you get to know a new stepparent. Concerns range from marrying too soon after divorce or a spouse's death, or too quickly following the initial date, to marrying someone of a different culture or religion. Perhaps you worry about a woman marrying Dad for his money or Mom marrying someone who is potentially abusive. Your attempts to persuade Mom or Dad to take the relationship slowly seemed to fall upon deaf ears. Mom or Dad is ecstatic about her or his forthcoming marriage, while your distress level rises.

The Possibility of Marriage

By their very nature, weddings are times to celebrate. Against all odds, two people have fallen in love and chosen to spend the rest of their lives together. They plan a ceremony in which they will commit to love, honor, and support each other. They may invite family and friends to witness the event. Like engaged couples of any age, they are happy and excited and they want others to share in their joy.

While it's hard to prepare for the unforeseen, just know that unexpected wedding announcements can and do happen. It's not unusual for older couples to have a short engagement of a few months or even weeks. Empirical data on dating and remarriage among the elderly is sparse; however, Dr. Sara Moorman reports in *The Journal of Family Issues*, "Widowed older people may . . . face a bind: their time perspective is reduced compared with young adults, yet the emotional reward of having a romantic partner may be great." Unlike younger betrothed couples who may need an engagement of months or a year in order to arrange schedules, save money, or make other plans, older couples often think a long betrothal is just a waste of time. Young newlyweds can anticipate a long future together, while older couples are less sure about the length of time they will have together.

Shauna expected her father to remarry after her mother died. She counseled him to keep her and her siblings informed. Her dad was less than forthcoming about his dating. Rumblings trickled through the sibling grapevine of their dad's romantic activities and rumored engagement. Shortly before his wedding, he invited Shauna to the ceremony. Even though she barely had enough time to make an airline reservation, she accepted gladly, although she did let her father know she would have preferred more warning. Shauna explained, "Parents are not obligated to inform their children of what they are doing and whom they are seeing—after all, it is their life and their business. However, we appreciate it." She was happy for her father and looked forward to the wedding and the chance to celebrate with her dad and new stepmother.

Recognizing the importance of the occasion and significance of future relationships, Shauna aptly chose to attend the ceremony offering support, love, and a hand of friendship. Rather than hiding her disappointment with her dad's lack of communication during his dating, Shauna discussed her feeling with her father and encouraged him to be more communicative of happenings affecting the family unit.

On the other hand, Richard's experience with his dad's wedding invitation was the opposite. As an only child, Richard would have been his father's only family member at the wedding. The two lived in different states and saw one another infrequently. Two weeks' notice was all that Richard received of his dad's wedding plans. Not only was Richard surprised, but he was also shocked since he was unaware that his dad had been dating. Because of family commitments and timing, Richard was unable to attend the wedding, "My father and his new wife wanted us to come for the wedding, but they really didn't give us adequate time. We had commitments that we couldn't get out of. Consequently, we didn't attend the wedding, and I think that caused some hard feelings. In retrospect, I wish I would have made more of an effort to attend, to be there for my dad." Subsequent conversations with his dad and stepmother gave Richard the impression that his absence hurt their feelings. He realized, too late, the value of rearranging schedules to support his father by attending his wedding. "That is one thing that I would do differently," he said.

Prior commitments may be difficult to rearrange, but as Richard learned, parents want your approval and support just as much as you desire theirs. Attending your parent's wedding when invited shows your love for your parent, acknowledges your stepparent as a member of your family, and represents a conscientious effort to support the marriage. Unity is but one of the possible rewards of rearranging schedules or flying in from out of town to help celebrate the new union.

Desires and Reactions

Have you considered the alternative—Mom or Dad remaining single? During a dental appointment, the dentist's assistant expressed to me her desire for her divorced parents of fifteen years to remarry. Well aware of their loneliness, she would like them to once again have a companion. She was surprised when

I told her that I was writing a book on the topic of remarriage, and she wondered why adult children struggle with their mom or dad marrying again. Two days later during a return appointment, the same assistant was anxious to share with me a conversation with her neighbor who experienced her mother's remarriage: "My neighbor said she was angry when her mom first remarried but later came to love and appreciate her stepdad for the happiness he brought to her mother. I asked her why she was angry, and her response was 'selfishness.'"

Cathy longed for her mother, who had been divorced for twenty-five years, to once again enjoy a marital relationship. Her mom met a recently divorced man on the Internet. One month later they were engaged and six weeks later married. Cathy was excited for them: "Mom's life revolved around her kids and grandkids. We became best friends. I knew she needed a companion. I encouraged them to marry quickly since they knew what they wanted and needed and didn't know how much time they would have together. I am happy for my mom and okay with her life revolving around her husband. She deserves to be happy with a companion."

Changing mores, increasing numbers of singles fifty and over, and the advent of the Internet that helps facilitate acquaintances result in an increased opportunity of marriage among the middle-aged and elderly. This may be good especially if you consider the advantages of marriage. Regardless of age, men and women are affected physically and psychologically by their marital status. For example, in their book *The Case for Marriage: Why Married People are Happier, Healthier, and Better Off Financially*, well-known sociologist Linda Waite and her associate report that, in general, people are happier and healthier in marital situations than those cohabiting or single. Remarriage fulfills the basic need of intimacy and companionship. It increases meaningfulness of involvement in society and offers a better quality of life by easing financial burdens and decreasing depression. Perhaps you have additional reasons to consider favorably the possibility of your parent's remarriage.

Examine Your Reactions

Sometimes it's hard to muster up genuine joy if you just heard about the pending nuptials a few days ago. Even as your parent is experiencing a new lift to life, you may be struggling with the suddenness of it. If your parent has been recently widowed or divorced, you probably think he or she is remarrying too hastily. You may still be grieving the loss of your parent. You may not have had time to adjust to your parent being single, let alone remarrying. Feeling deprived of the chance to help plan such a life-changing event can make you withdraw further. It's not uncommon to feel that your parent is being disloyal to the memory of a deceased parent by remarrying so quickly—or at all. Some children—even adult children—feel a sense of loneliness or abandonment. There may be a concern that your parent is rushing into something that may not be in his or her best interest. None of these perceptions is likely to make you feel like celebrating.

Your life may be reeling because of your parent's divorce or the shock of the sudden death of your mom or dad. Feelings of guilt may plague you for not spending more time with them or for not preventing the divorce. Anger wells within you, directed at everyone and yet no one. At times you would give anything for just a day or even a few minutes to spend with your deceased parent or to return to the previous normality of family life. Instead, the reality of your parent's absence confronts you, and your resulting feelings can affect all aspects of your life if not resolved. Guilt, anger, or other feelings may be the root cause of your emotional reaction to Mom dating or to Dad's wedding announcement. Sometimes the dating partner or fiancé(e) becomes the focus of misdirected anger and the victim of misjudgments and false accusations. How unfair!

A **Stepparent's** Perspective

When Anne married Neal, she recognized that two of his four children probably needed more time before he remarried. Neal's other two children were more comfortable with his new marriage because they lived close by and helped care for their mother during her illness. They grieved for her as they watched her health deteriorate. They saw firsthand their father's loneliness and his discomfort in social situations. They also witnessed the change in him that occurred as his relationship developed with Anne. Seeing all this helped them to accept Neal and Anne's marriage.

For example, Patricia had two aunts die suddenly within a short time of each other. Their widowed husbands remarried within a year. Patricia's cousins, furious and angry, were "mean" to their stepmothers. Was it the stepmothers' fault that the mothers died? No, of course not. Yet, they became the target of the children's attacks. Patricia said that the children in one family now love their stepmother and call her "blessed" for the happiness she gives to their father and them. They now see the folly of their misguided behavior.

Perhaps you have allowed your emotions to control your behavior. Consider permitting your behavior to affect your emotions as Shauna did. On the way to her dad's wedding, Shauna told a woman on the plane that she felt like an orphan. With her mother gone, she felt her father's new wife would become his priority, leaving her out completely. It's extreme, but a parent remarrying may make you feel as though you've lost both parents. This feeling may appear contradictory to

Shauna's happiness for her father. However, closer scrutiny reveals that one emotion (happiness) is related to her concerns for her dad's welfare, while her orphaned feeling comes from her personal sense of loss of the family she knew. Shauna chose to be happy and to celebrate with her dad and new stepmother rather than letting loneliness consume her.

Therapist Debra McGill offered this advice for Shauna's dilemma or similar situations: "It's important to acknowledge your feelings honestly. Maybe even write them down. I give clients the assignment of writing a 'letter' to the person they're having feelings about—it may be the parent or the stepparent. This puts the writing in the first person: 'I feel abandoned and left out by this sudden decision.' This is not a letter meant to be sent. It's just helpful to force yourself to find the words that describe your feelings accurately." This is one method of helping you examine and understand emotional reactions and subsequent behaviors.

Find Reasons to Rejoice

Couples I interviewed seemed truly happy in their marriage. They found joy being together. Marriage enriches their lives because they have someone with whom they can share the simple pleasures of life. Life is again meaningful when widowed or divorced parents have someone to love, to care for, and to enjoy. Though engulfed with feelings of grief or anger, many adult children found reasons to rejoice with their parent's remarriage. For some the rejoicing came years after the wedding. Eventually they recognized the happiness, good health, or social associations it provided their mom or dad. Why wait years to rejoice? Appreciate these blessings in your parent's life during the courtship and prepare to celebrate on their wedding day.

Happiness

After her father's quick remarriage, Kristen discussed her concerns with a friend. The friend shared this bit of wisdom: 'If somebody has been happily married, that person tends to get married again relatively quickly." Without knowing it, Kristen's wise friend echoed Samuel Johnson, writing in the eighteenth century: "By taking a second wife, [a man] pays the highest compliment to the first, by showing that she made him so happy as a married man that he wishes to be so a second time." Kristen was grateful for the insight, because it acknowledged the relationship between her mother and father. It allowed her to rejoice in her dad's renewed happiness and accept her stepmother as a friend, rather than to see her as a replacement for her mother.

Kristen felt that her parents had a good marriage. She felt secure in familial love. It has been said, "The most important thing a father can do for his children is to love their mother." If your parents had a happy marriage, let your widowed parent's decision to wed again reaffirm your conviction. Rejoice in the newfound happiness that your mom or dad is experiencing, and welcome your stepparent as a friend.

A **Parent's** Perspective

Kristen's dad, Nick, said, "If children have respect for or any love for their parents, hope and pray that they find a companion with whom they can continue living the life they used to live. Because my first wife and I had a very blissful life, never an argument, I was happy being married. I am a happy man again."

What if the first marriage wasn't all that happy? Even small children see through a fake smile or their parents' attempts to feign happiness while they internally suffer heartbreak and anguish. Often, the divorce is no surprise and may even be a welcome relief of bitterness, hostility, or general apathy. If this exemplifies your family, life certainly didn't hand you the ideal scenario. Now you have the choice of making the best of an undesirable situation.

Cathy's mom was twice divorced, the second time after less than a year while pregnant with her youngest child. Twenty-five years later Cathy was thrilled for her sixty-something-year-old mother to have a romantic interest: "It is her turn to experience happiness after many years of being single." Cathy had her mother's welfare at heart when she celebrated her mom and Howard's wedding with them.

However, not all family members were happy. Howard's daughter, Candy, from his second marriage was noticeably absent from the wedding. Still angry about her parents' divorce, Candy refused to attend the ceremony and has no intention of meeting her new stepmother. It seems as though Candy has no desire or reason to rejoice.

Candy has a choice to continue to take the attitude of "woe is me" or seek professional counseling to work through her feelings.

If a first or second marriage was unhappy, some people continue to search for the marital happiness they failed to achieve previously. As an adult child, you may refuse or may not want to recognize the unhappiness of the union that produced you. Or you may feel that your parent is bashing his or her deceased or divorced spouse. One possible cause is the reactivation of similar feelings originating during childhood.

Regardless of your attitude regarding your parent's engagement, let his or her happiness permeate your thoughts, and appreciate this blessing the new companion gives your parent.

Health

Add to happiness good health, and what more could you ask for your parents throughout their senior years? Researchers have found a positive correlation between a good marriage and good health for people of all ages.

Kristen noticed the dramatic improvement in her father's health beginning with his return to social involvement. Kristen watched her father's loving care for her mother throughout her debilitative disease. Kristen also noticed a change in her dad's health, which continued to decline after her mother's death. His health perked up when he began playing bridge with widows, followed by dating and his eventual marriage to Mary. Kristen attributes her dad's extended life (eighty-seven years) to Mary, "After my mother died, my dad was totally lost. He looked like he would be dead in a few months. I believe Mary saved his life. After Mom died, Dad was lonely. Without a companion he would have given up."

Children can only do so much for parents. You can invite them to dinner, for celebrations, or to join you on vacations. For a few minutes or a few days Mom enjoys spending time with her grandchildren and spoiling them. Dad makes the perfunctory visit but often feels uncomfortable without his companion. At the conclusion of each activity, Mom or Dad returns to their empty house—a reminder of her or his loneliness. The silence seems to echo through every room: *You're by yourself now.* Some enjoy the solitude and discover latent talents or pursue old or new hobbies, but many experience intense feelings of loneliness.

Elderly parents dating and desiring an intimate companion are in the minority of their age group. Your parent's dating provides an opportunity for you to view Mom or Dad from a different perspective. You discover they are similar to young people entering the dating stage or to young engaged couples. Dr. Joyce Brothers said, "Studies prove that falling in love feels the same whether you're 15 or 50. The need to connect with one another intimately is what makes and keeps us human. The challenge throughout life is to find the courage to reach out to potential new partners when our primary relationship ends."

Melanie's mom suffered from depression following her husband's death. Her mom saw a doctor for depression and even tried a face-lift thinking that would lift her spirits. Several years later her mom started attending dances and conferences for older singles and "began to have a ball dating and receiving flowers, gifts, and even proposals." Melanie noticed a marked improvement in her mother's health—the depression was replaced by laughter and lightheartedness.

Melanie noted that she was a young, single mom when her father died. Enveloped by her personal challenges, Melanie didn't think to check on her mother: "I didn't talk to her and ask how she was feeling. I didn't call her to see if she was doing okay." Now with teenagers and adult children of her own, Melanie recognizes the importance of doing the little things to check on parents or others. The seemingly trivial behaviors—a phone call, visit, e-mail, or letter—let parents know you are thinking about them and concerned about their welfare. An awareness of your parent's physical and emotional struggles during widowhood helps you appreciate the improved health and mental outlook accompanying a new romance—another reason to rejoice on their wedding day.

Improved Quality of Life

The termination of a marital relationship either by death or divorce impacts the social networks of the spouses. In my clinical experience with divorced men and women, I have found that their contacts with friends they had as a couple decrease dramatically during the year following their divorce. After a year, men typically begin developing new contacts through involvement in social clubs or organizations and women become more involved with family.

Melanie's stepdad, Dan, provided her mom with a change of lifestyle that only a companion can. Her parents' marriage reached a point of monotony—work, dinner, TV, and bed—as some marriages do when spouses fail to infuse them with hobbies, dating, or social activities. Her mom's relationship with Dan is quite opposite. They engage in ballroom and square dancing and in religious and local community activities. "It was refreshing for Mom, and it made me happy to see her have a different lifestyle," Melanie said.

Trudie remembers her parents doing things socially when she was a child, and then saw their social interaction wane as she moved into adolescence and adulthood. Her stepmother is younger than her mother was and in better health. Trudie reminisced, "My dad and his new wife are more socially involved than my parents were. They volunteer for their church and meet other couples their age with whom they occasionally go out to eat, visit, and have even vacationed together. My dad enjoys traveling, so he appreciates his wife's good health, which allows her to accompany him on trips and various other activities."

How does this affect you as an adult child? The nature of your relationship with your parents changes following divorce or the death of one. Interaction with dads usually diminishes, while it increases with moms. Dads tend to be independent, finding something to keep themselves busy, whether it be immersing themselves in their work, hanging out at the gym or on the golf course, or joining a club. They rarely ask for help with challenges or discuss them until they have a solution. On the other hand, moms tend to be needier than their counterpart, relying on family for emotional and social support. They call more frequently to check on you, but probably for the social interaction. They find reasons to join your family for a picnic, a recital, or other family activity to remain an active part of the group. Thus, interaction with your father may diminish while it increases with your mom. Based on research published in *Marriage and Family Review*, sociologist Terri L. Orbuch concluded, "While divorce without remarriage hurts sons' relationships with both fathers and mothers, it hurts father-daughter relations even more, while at the same time improving mother-daughter bonds." Sons may feel Mom should be more independent, while daughters are more understanding of Mom's need for companionship and are more willing to supply it.

Remarriage solves the problem of loneliness—a new marital companion sometimes works miracles. Dads come out of their cave and feel more comfortable in familial settings. Dad's new wife may even encourage him to interact more with you or to offer help with projects. You may discover abilities you never knew your dad possessed. With a new husband, Mom is less needy emotionally. She may be too busy to call every day. And that's okay. You no longer have to be available at her beck and call. As a couple, they may find new interests or rekindle forgotten leisure pleasures, all of which broadens their social contacts and improves their quality of life—another reason to rejoice with them on their wedding day and look forward to enriching relationships.

Financial Benefits

Citing previous studies, sociologist Ken R. Smith says, "Remarriage is one of the most important determinants of . . . economic well-being among the widowed."

Many elderly are on a fixed income, relying solely upon Social Security benefits. Of course, their economic well-being declines when one spouse dies, extinguishing half or more of their income. Others may receive pensions from retirement accounts that may also cease due to death. Their bills continue to arrive month after month. Add to that medication expenses and no wonder many struggle with buying essential food items. Yet the majority of widows and widowers want to live independently, unlike their parents who more often lived with family during their golden years. Remarriage once again provides two incomes, even though they might be meager, and at the same time the couple cuts monthly bills in half. You begin to see another advantage of remarriage; it allows Mom or Dad to remain independent with increased disposable income. Just one more reason to rejoice on their wedding day.

Sandy's mom and stepdad, Dean, live on fixed incomes. When they married, Dean sold his house to move into his new wife's home, and they combined their incomes. Sandy said they have enjoyed their time together and have even been able to save money for trips. They are better off financially together than they would be separately.

Kristen marvels at her stepmother, Mary, for working and supporting her four children after her first husband died at a young age. Single moms often struggle with finances while doing their best to raise well-adjusted, responsible children. Kristen and her siblings wondered if Mary might have ulterior motives for marrying their financially well-off dad. They soon learned that Mary truly loves their dad. The two enjoy each other's company, socializing, taking extended trips, and visiting family scattered across the states. (Financial challenges confronting adult children will be discussed more extensively in a later chapter.)

"Marrieds' greater economic resources and access to an intimate partner account for much of their advantage in psychological well-being," says sociologist Susan L. Brown in a research article published in the *Journal of Gerontology*. It is interesting that finances, health, and psychological well-being tie in closely with marriage. A steady income (though it may be modest), good health, and a good marriage promote emotional stability. Take one of these factors away and all other aspects of life are affected, usually adversely. If you love Mom and Dad and want them to stick around for a while, then remarriage is reason to celebrate.

Fewer Worries

In her book *Family Ties and Aging,* sociologist Dr. Connidis says, "Remarriage in later life has the potential for enhancing relations with children, who may now feel less burden, responsibility, or guilt, knowing that their parent is cared for by a spouse." You may have noticed increased contact with your divorced or widowed parents. You wonder how Mom is doing emotionally. Does she need help with household repairs? What about Dad? Is he eating enough of the right things? Though he says he is all right, is he really okay? Will they take themselves to the doctor when they are sick? What if they fall and get hurt? Will anyone know to help them? Worry prompts you to call more frequently or stop by on your way home from work just to make sure things are okay. And you should worry: according to a 2006 article published on the Population Reference Bureau's Web site, "White men over the age of 65 commit suicide at almost triple the overall U.S. rate—and almost twice the rate of any other group." Checking on parents is easy when they live close by, but issues are complicated when they live further away.

A **Stepparent's** Perspective

Mary said, "Children should look at the big picture and not just the money angle, which is what they usually look at first if any money is involved. And don't think of a remarriage as someone trying to replace a parent but as someone to help your living parent have a happy, wonderful life with God's blessing."

Advantages of your parent's remarriage include having a companion, a helper, and a caregiver. If both your parent and stepparent are in good health, they can enjoy life together. Moms appreciate having someone to make repairs, while dads appreciate having someone to take care of household chores. For the sixty-plus generation the delineation of household chores is still common. Any physical problem becomes less of a burden for you knowing that Mom or Dad's spouse is caring for her or him. Of course, you are still concerned about your parent's health, but it is reassuring knowing that Mom or Dad has a companion who loves her or him and is there in case of emergency.

Every decade of life seems to bring with it physical changes and health concerns, which increase throughout the senior years. Another companion relieves some of your worries about your parents' welfare, since married couples tend to eat better, watch out for their health, and receive proper health care. When your parent is married, peace of mind replaces worry because you know someone else is in the house.

Since Richard lived several hundred miles from his father, it was difficult for him to be available if his father needed help. Richard was happy to learn that his dad was engaged: "Dad was all alone." If anything happened to his dad, Richard knew that his new stepmother would provide care until he could arrive if necessary.

Your stepparent is a blessing in your life by being a companion, a helper, and a caregiver to your parent. Worries and concerns diminish just knowing someone is in the house with Mom or Dad. You are not called for every faucet leak or burned-out light bulb. Above all, someone helps assure medications are taken and health care is received. Consider these three reasons to rejoice at the wedding. Rather than feeling as though you're losing a parent, consider the wedding day as an opportunity to make a new friend.

Take Action

Some parents refrain from telling children of their romances for fear of their disapproval. In fact, some adult children surprise themselves by their reaction to a parent's repartnering activities. Here are some suggestions for mastering negative responses.

Experiences elicit emotional responses. Acknowledge initial reactions as a first impression. Allow yourself time to adjust to the idea of Mom or Dad remarrying.

Examine your feelings behind the reaction. Perhaps the root of the problem extends to childhood experiences, to fear of rejection, or to selfishness. Separate the root cause from the symptom, and deal with each appropriately.

Make a conscious effort to determine your reaction. Choose to be happy and to act in a loving, accepting manner until those feelings are natural.

Possible Scenario

This can be a period of self-reflection to examine your feelings, motives, and desires. Ask yourself the following questions and answer them truthfully: What am I feeling? Anger. Betrayal. Confusion. Why am I feeling this way? Dad told me he wouldn't remarry. I thought Mom and Dad were happy and would work out their differences. I want more time with Mom or Dad to work through the grieving process. What kind of relationship do I desire? I desire to be miserable and make others miserable. I desire to be happy and develop loving relationships. How can I change my situation? I can change my attitude. I can try to understand my parent's behavior. I can make the effort to support my parent and become acquainted with his or her companion. I can change how I view this situation by seeing that it has the potential to add a new supportive relationship, not one that will replace Mom or Dad, but one that will build my support system.

The Heart of the Matter

Perhaps you wondered how you can feel sad yet relieved at the same time about the pending wedding of your mom or dad. Ambivalent feelings often accompany significant changes in life. Your parent's remarriage can be classified as a significant change. Accept the feelings as normal and determine your desired behavior, which will build a secure bond.

- If your parent is dating, consider the possibility that he or she may remarry. Even if no wedding has been announced, it will give you some time to get used to the idea! Recognize that your parent is not trying to replace your mom or dad. That can never happen. Rather, they are beginning a new relationship that does not have to threaten either your parent's or your loyalty to your deceased parent.
- If you strongly disapprove of the marriage or future stepparent, take the time to examine your emotions, motives, and desires. Why do you feel that way? Is your disapproval rooted in fact or perception? Accept that it's your parent's choice. If necessary, try to discuss your concerns with your parent.
- Consider the wedding day as a lease on new life for your parent—happiness, health, social activity, financial improvement, freedom from loneliness—or as an opportunity for you to make new friends or as a relief of worry. That alone is a reason to rejoice!

CHAPTER 4

To Attend or Not to Attend the Wedding?

"Every decision you make—every decision—is not a decision about what to do. It's a decision about Who You Are. When you see this, when you understand it, everything changes. You begin to see life in a new way. All events, occurrences, and situations turn into opportunities to do what you came here to do."
—*Neale Donald Walsch*

For better or for worse, your parent's wedding day has arrived. Perhaps you were included in the planning and invited to be in the wedding party, or you were excluded altogether. Each affects your current and future relationship with your parent and stepparent as well as your decision to attend the ceremony. Consider carefully the consequences of your choice. Though you will not be saying "I do" to the nuptial vows, your presence or absence at the wedding indicates your commitment to love and honor your parent and his or her new spouse.

The Pain of Exclusion

The need to feel included in social groups is a defining human characteristic. If you feel excluded from the wedding preparations or ceremony itself, you could suffer very real pain. At the University of California, Los Angeles, Dr. Naomi I. Eisenberger conducted studies of social exclusion and wrote about her findings in the journal *Science*. She looked at how the brain and body respond to the emotional pain of exclusion, whether initiated by others or by extenuating circumstance, and found that "the pain of exclusion, felt as social rejection, registers in the same part of the brain as physical pain." Dr. Eisenberger's research highlights the integral need for social connection that we all feel. Exclusion can feel as painful as a blow, and just as life threatening. Such pain can affect the family relationship into the future if not acknowledged and dealt with.

Regardless of his intentions, the actions of Trudie's father, Lance, hurt her. Lance had been reluctant to tell her he was dating. When he told her about his wedding just two weeks before the day, Trudie said, "I felt like an outsider rather than a daughter." She began to wonder what role she had in her father's new family, which now included stepsiblings. Every time she heard about a family dinner to which she hadn't been invited, the pain of exclusion caused Trudie to distance herself even further from her father and his new wife. She described what she felt as a very real pain in her chest.

Trudie tried to overlook her dad's behavior but relived it every time another exclusion occurred. Rather than confronting her dad and sharing her feelings, Trudie made no attempt to contact or visit him and gave perfunctory cordiality when he called her. Perhaps her pain would dissipate if she stayed away. She said that perhaps he would understand how deeply she hurt if he felt the same way, but said, "Instead, I learned that doing wrong never makes you feel better but only worsens the problem. My actions accomplished the intent of hurting my dad but did nothing to alleviate my pain." Like the old adage says, "Two wrongs don't make a right." Avoidance of problems or misunderstanding only prolongs the eventual confrontation. Sooner or later Trudie needs to discuss her feelings with her dad in a nonconfrontational way so they both feel understood. The second step is to mutually decide on a solution to the problem. Trudie could be prepared with a couple of solutions she is willing to live with. A sincere, open discussion brings awareness to the problem and an understanding of the side effects of specific behaviors. The third step would be to implement the solution, thus relieving the hurt and avoiding any repeat mistakes.

A **Parent's** Perspective

In some circumstances, your parent may try to discourage you from attending the wedding. Perhaps your father understands the trip would be a financial burden on you, or your mother realizes you just can't get away that month. That was the case with Nick, who didn't want to burden his daughter, Kristen, or any of the other children, with travel expenses to the civil wedding. He and Mary were planning a church wedding later near many of the family members and it was more important that the family be together for that event. He had a good reason for keeping the civil ceremony private.

In another family, Steve recognized the hurt his new stepsisters must have felt during the wedding reception for his mom, Shirley, and their dad, Nolan. When the photographer announced a family picture, Nolan's daughters and their families could not be found. No one had invited them specifically to be in the picture, so they had assumed they were excluded.

Their already tenuous relationship with Nolan was weakened further as a result.

Apparently, exclusion of Steve's stepsisters was not intended. False assumptions occur frequently, resulting in psychological pain. Nevertheless, the pain is real and must be considered. After the fact, Shirley and Nolan could apologize for the misunderstanding and offer to have family pictures retaken. In which case, the daughters should graciously accept their apology and overlook the incident as a simple misunderstanding. Before the fact, the girls could have approached their dad and Shirley and asked if they were to be included. A warm embrace and positive assurance would have avoided the problem.

If similar situations confront you, first and foremost, check your assumptions. A majority of misunderstandings would never occur if dialogue were included. If you do make assumptions, give Mom or Dad and your stepparent the benefit of the doubt. Most would not intentionally try to hurt you. For example, assume you are wanted in the picture since you are a member of the family. If you are intentionally excluded, then you definitely have a problem and want to consider carefully how you proceed with your interactions.

For example, Sarah also experienced exclusionary pain when her father remarried, remarking, "It makes a huge difference how much parents include you right from the beginning." Inclusion in wedding plans or the wedding party reaffirms your parent's love for you and a desire for you to remain an active part of his or her life and new union. Acceptance wells within you just like a well-earned A on an English paper, encouraging you to put forth your best effort to support the marriage. On the other hand, exclusion causes doubt of your parent's love and your role in his or her new family. It also shows favoritism, resulting in a division among the children. Contrast the feeling of acceptance with the feeling of rejection, another common dilemma Dr. Corrie has recognized among her adult stepchild clientele. You may put forth some effort to build a relationship, but future rejections eventually squelch your desire to become friends.

Several years after her parents divorced, Sarah's father met Lois and they eventually married. Sarah's family was excluded from the beginning of her father's new relationship. "Lois's children were in the wedding party, but we weren't. It was divisive." Sarah still feels the pain, even though many years have passed since his remarriage and several years since his death. Exclusion weakened her relationship with her father and stepmother. Sarah attempted to overlook it and frequently invited her dad and Lois to her family's activities and athletic events. On the rare occasions they accepted the invitations, Sarah sensed uneasiness in Lois and an anxiousness to leave. In spite of the rejection, Sarah recognized the problem as her stepmother's pessimism about developing a loving relationship and continued inviting them. How much rejection are you obligated to endure before you quit trying?

Moving beyond pain requires your effort. Therapist Debra McGill offers these suggestions: "You could talk about it with a trusted friend, sibling, or therapist; write about it as before outlined; read books about overcoming pain." Many therapists would encourage you to change how you view the situation, which will help you work through the pain. The important point is that you can take control and do something about it.

Sarah's mother had a different attitude, and her actions produced a different outcome. "My mother made an effort from the beginning to include both sides in the wedding party. You can't control feelings, but you can control situations, like helping stepchildren feel welcome or equal." Sarah added that her mother has maintained a good relationship with her stepchildren because she reached out to them and included them.

If your parent invites you to participate in the wedding plans, recognize that he or she is trying to be fair and prevent hurt feelings. It sets a tone of equality for the two families joined by the new marriage. It helps you begin to feel comfortable with your new stepparent and reaffirms your importance in the new family structure.

Some couples plan two ceremonies to accommodate all the children in the two families. A justice of the peace married Kristen's dad, Nick, and Mary in a small ceremony attended only by Mary's son and daughter-in-law. Later the couple had a church wedding and mass, which all the family attended to rejoice and celebrate with them.

Share the Joy

It may sound surprising, but parents often want the approval of their children just as much as children want the approval of their parents. Attending the wedding is one way to show your love for your parent and to acknowledge his or her new spouse. You may have had short notice, you may not approve of your parent's choice, or you may live a long distance away, but being present for the wedding indicates your effort to accept the marriage and your willingness to be a part of this new union.

Mike and his six siblings were told of their father's wedding shortly before the date, but all of them were in attendance. "We wanted dad to know that we would be there for him." Some lived nearby; others flew in from across the country. Their dad always tried to be there for their special events and to help in whatever way he could. Now it was Mike and his siblings' turn to reciprocate. Mike's father and new wife felt—and saw—that all of the children supported their marriage. Physical presence doesn't always indicate emotional support. Mike said that some of his siblings took awhile to warm up to their stepmother and some have yet to embrace her, but they showed love and support by attending the nuptials.

A **Parent's** Perspective

Four of the five combined children of Marie and John were okay with their marriage. Marie said, "To remain alone the rest of your life because one child doesn't see eye-to-eye doesn't make sense. I would be sitting alone in my lonely, old house while my children live their lives."

Extenuating circumstances or undesirable feelings may keep you from giving emotional support, but a physical presence communicates goodwill and indicates personal effort to acknowledge their joy even if you don't share it.

Pressing business, prior commitments, or other circumstances may keep you away, but know that not attending the wedding when invited, for whatever reason, could be interpreted by your parent or stepparent as a lack of interest or acceptance on your part. Such misunderstandings can affect your relationship with one or both of them. It's worth the effort to rearrange your schedule to be present.

Richard lamented, "I think my absence from the wedding caused some hard feelings." Nancy's children attended the ceremony in support of their mom, while Richard's dad was bereft of familial support.

Remember, it's never too late for an apology. They may not need one, but you will feel better having given one. Expressing your regret "clears the air." Also, it is the responsibility of the soon-to-be-married parent to communicate to the children if he or she has a strong desire for them to attend. Richard may have made more of an effort if he had known it was important to his dad. If you are truly unable to accept an invitation to attend the ceremony, do your best to explain your situation. Send a card or gift to acknowledge the event. Call them later to offer your congratulations and to discuss the details of the day. Plan a time to visit them, especially if you have yet to meet your stepparent.

Wedding Etiquette

This very important day in your family is the perfect opportunity to act like the adult you are, regardless of anything that has gone on before. You are your parent's child, but that doesn't give you license to act like one.

Sandy admitted to some childish tendencies on her mother's wedding day. "I asked my mom where they were going on their honeymoon. Dean wanted it kept a secret, so mom wouldn't tell me. Later I found out that she had told my sisters. I was not happy—I felt left out." It was two months before Sandy talked to her mother again. By then, she realized her childishness. "She's a woman, not just my mother. Her life is her life."

And once you are there at the wedding, make a conscientious decision to smile—and mean it. There are many very real reasons to rejoice. Your mom or dad now has a companion who gives new meaning to life. Loneliness has been replaced with companionship. Your parent is happy, and has someone to care for, and to care for them in return. Mom or Dad told you about the wedding and invited you! You can probably think of others. Think how you would like people to act at your wedding and do the same. Let your parent's engagement and special day be filled with happiness. In her book *A Revolution in Kindness*, author Anita Roddick reminds us, "The end result of kindness is that it draws people to you."

Find the Humor

The humorist Will Rogers once said, "Everything is funny as long as it is happening to someone else." You don't need to be a standup comedian to find the humor in uncomfortable situations. Weddings come with stress—it's a fact of life. Emotions run high. Comments that would be brushed aside as insignificant any other time can be blown way out of proportion. The most innocent or thoughtless remarks can spark a feud that would do the Hatfields and McCoys proud unless you keep your sense of humor firmly intact.

Anyone who has siblings has at some point been called the wrong name by a parent. In an especially large family, an overworked mom may need to run down the list of names before remembering the right one! Presumably, you don't take offense, and why would you at such an innocent slip?

Somehow it seems different when a stepparent does it. Suddenly it seems as if he or she doesn't care enough about you to even learn your name. You feel less inclined to cut your stepparent the same slack. But when you stop and think about it, perhaps you have spent very little time with this person. Maybe you have lots of siblings and the family resemblance among you is strong. Unless you want to wear nametags, know that slip-ups will happen.

Stacey felt deeply hurt when her new stepmother, Phyllis, called her by her sister Shauna's name. In her mind, this woman, now a member of the family, didn't know them well enough—or perhaps even care—to tell them apart. Stacey managed to conceal her feelings, but her stepmother's credibility suffered in her eyes.

Feelings of insecurity or loss of self-esteem may result from wedding-day gaffes. These feelings could be new or reactivated from childhood. A good sense of humor is one way to deal with feelings of insecurity. Put the faux pas in perspective and isolate it from you as an individual.

Kristen recalled her uncle's toast at her father's wedding, during which he called Mary by Nick's first wife's name. "He was devastated, but Mary was just as gracious as she could be." When Mary made a joke out of the incident, Kristen was impressed: "I thought it showed how secure she is." She was also touched by the way that Mary tried to learn everyone's names, including all nine of Nick's children, their spouses, and their children, as well as birthdays. "Mary made a conscientious effort. That's the type of person she is." Mary's effort went a long way toward building credibility in her new stepfamily's eyes.

In an effort to express love and acceptance, some stepparents may call you "daughter" or "son." Of course you aren't his or her child. The word may not even describe the type of relationship you want to have with this person. When Helen embraced her new stepdaughter, Trudie, she said, "Thank you, daughter." Trudie said that she felt her whole body stiffen and knew that Helen noticed. Her thoughts raced, *You haven't done anything to presume to be my mother. I haven't done anything worthy of being called daughter. I have a mother even though she is dead. I don't need another mother. I don't want another mother.* She withheld the urge to say it wasn't okay, even though it was obvious to both of them that Trudie wasn't comfortable with the term.

Rather than taking offense, recognize that saying this is a way for your stepparent to show love and acceptance. Melanie recalled that the first time Chuck introduced her as "our daughter" it felt a bit unsettling, but now she recognizes it as a term of endearment, a way of expressing love, and she rather likes it.

Such situations will happen. It's up to you to decide how you're going to react to them. Find the humor if you can. "Humor brings insight and tolerance," notes Agnes Repplier in her book *In Pursuit of Laughter*. Both Stacey's stepmother and Kristen's uncle had the best of intentions. If other emotions, such as anger or resentment, are boiling beneath the surface, even the most insignificant slips can produce overreactions. If you remember not to take them personally, you can let them slip by just as easily as they slipped out.

Autonomy Versus Shame

To understand this phase of your relationship, picture a toddler between eighteen months and four years of age. She exudes exuberance dressing herself, buttoning her coat, tying her shoes, singing the ABCs. She develops autonomy through her newfound control. The independent "Me do it!" is often accompanied with stubbornness or negativism as she exercises her prerogative to say "No!" As an adult observing your parent and stepparent's relationship, perhaps you've learned new skills of withholding judgment, controlling your tongue, or behaving civilly. Rather than acting independently of your parents, you act independently of your emotions that want to resist this new marriage. Or perhaps you've let the negativism slip out as you've tried to force your opinions on your parent. "Me do it" may be cute for a toddler, but the attitude of "I won't support this marriage" is unbecoming in an adult—and ultimately you are the one who suffers.

Take Action

Let's examine one scenario from this chapter and discuss specific actions you can take to change the outcome. Recall Sarah's exclusion from her dad's wedding party. Feelings of rejection are definitely undesirable and may cause continuous problems if left unresolved. The first consideration is to try to avoid them.

- If the wedding is to take place near where you live and you are aware of it in advance, offer to help by addressing invitations, making phone calls, using a talent such as decorating a cake or making a floral arrangement, or helping with decorations.
- If your offers are rejected and they continue to exclude you, try to ignore it. Brush it aside as an unintentional

67

faux pas. Look for the silver lining, like being grateful you don't have to purchase an expensive gown or rent a tuxedo.

- If those fail and you continue to feel rejected by ongoing behaviors, try to discuss the issue with your parent and stepparent and come up with a solution acceptable to everyone.
- If the act or gaffe was intentional or malicious, you're dealing with someone who has a serious personality flaw. Don't expect to be able to change them, and don't sink to their level. Be the good person you want to be no matter what they say or do to you.

Possible Scenario

You've just learned that your dad is engaged. You want your future stepmother to know that you are willing to help with the plans or arrangements of the wedding.

Child: My dad just told me the good news. Congratulations on your forthcoming marriage.

Stepparent: Thank you.

Child: You must be busy planning all the details. Is there something I can do to help you?

Stepparent: We've decided to have a simple ceremony without a wedding party, so not much planning is involved.

Child: One of my hobbies is floral decorating. I would love to make your wedding bouquet for you.

Stepparent: Thanks for your offer, but our family tradition is for the bride to carry three red roses.

Child: Am I at least invited to the wedding?

Stepparent: Of course you are. Your attendance will mean so much to your father and to me.

The Heart of the Matter

The inevitable, surprising, or even shocking wedding day has arrived. Perhaps you knew that marriage was always a possibility for your single parent, but you chose not to think about it. Now you are forced to consider a remarriage and how it affects you and your parent.

- Don't distance yourself, even if you feel excluded. Reach out to your parent and future stepparent—and sooner rather than later. The longer you cling to resentment, the harder it will be to make the effort.
- Try to attend your parent's wedding, no matter how short the notice. Ceremonies serve an important purpose of bonding, and rejecting an invitation will be remembered for a long time. If they opt for a private ceremony, respect their wishes. Find a special gift or other way to recognize this important event and make the new spouse feel welcome. You do this more for you than for them.
- Help make the day as happy as possible. Weddings can be stressful, so make an effort to alleviate the anxiety, rather than add to it.
- If someone makes a gaffe, be gracious. Overlook the unintentional mistakes of others just as you would like them to overlook yours. Consider your words before you react to avoid hurting anyone's feelings. It may take awhile for a new spouse to put the correct name with each face, especially if the family is large. Be patient and help your stepparent out.

CHAPTER 5

"I Don't Feel Comfortable Calling You 'Dad'"

"The happiest and most successful people all share . . . the ability to quickly adapt to new situations and circumstances . . . to go with the flow and not only accept change but embrace it as an opportunity to expand yourself and your life."
—*T. Harv Eker*

The wedding is over. You survived the faux pas and glitches, the laughter and tears, and learned something along the way about the charms and idiosyncrasies of the new people in your life. Now comes the challenging part: finding your place in this new marital union.

Even as your parent settles into a new but familiar role as husband or wife, his or her core relationship with you hasn't changed. You are still that person's child and nothing can change that. What will probably change is some of your interaction with your parent, its frequency and nature. The new significant other is going to take up a good deal of your parent's time and attention—and that may be time and attention you were accustomed to getting.

71

With the return to the single life, your mom or dad had time to focus on you and your family. Perhaps you and Mom have become best friends. You enjoy your adult conversation with her and perhaps seek her motherly wisdom concerning child rearing. Or maybe you enjoy girls' night out with her, playing doubles in tennis, attending a book club, or simply window-shopping and giggling. Dad has had more time to attend athletic events or recitals. His encouraging word or a pat on the back seems to mean more to your son or daughter than your words. His presence offers support to you and your children.

Will your relationship stay the same? Maybe not. Is it appropriate to spend alone time with your parent? Of course. Should you talk about your absent parent in front of the new spouse? Such situations require sensitivity on your part. As you settle into your new role, you make adjustments. It may feel like sending your oldest child to kindergarten or to college. Your house is quieter and your life lonelier for a few hours or months until your child returns. Just as your college-bound child was ready and excited for a new adventure, so is your parent. Or remember the first time you left home and experienced some disconnection in your relationships with Mom and Dad. You regarded them more as a confidante, friend, and advisor rather than as a parent telling you what to do. All adapted to your new roles. Once again, you adjust and know that change is part of life's progression. A new normalcy replaces the old and you appreciate your time together. Even though your relationship with your parent is different, you will become comfortable with it.

The moment your parent said, "I do," you became someone's stepchild, too. The role of stepchild may be foreign to you. It can feel awkward and may cause you anxiety. You may also have new stepsiblings and all of the family connections that they bring to the mix. Learning how to adapt to these new and unfamiliar roles can relieve some of your anxiety. As always, consideration, thoughtfulness, and a sense of humor will help you, too. It's time to discover your new supporting—and supportive—role in your parent and stepparent's life.

My Mom, the Newlywed

Newlyweds of any age need time alone to nurture their new relationship. You aren't the only one trying to figure out things. Be considerate of your parent and stepparent and let them have some uninterrupted time together to focus on each other.

Changing Roles

Your role as child has been evolving throughout your life, from the time you were a helpless infant who looked to your parents to fulfill your every need, to adolescence and adulthood, as you developed your independence and struck out on your own. This evolution is most noticeable when major changes occur, and a parent's remarriage certainly qualifies as a "major change." It's natural to want to feel that you're still important to your mom or dad. You desire to make sure you're still loved, needed, and a part of the family. Diane felt left out after her mother's remarriage: "My mom and Jim live their lives. If we happen to fit in somewhere then that's fine, but whatever they are doing is the priority. The family is second to that." Diane's mother had been her biggest supporter throughout her life. Her support was no longer guaranteed. What do you do when the warranty has expired and you have a problem? Understandably, the adjustment has been challenging for Diane.

Perhaps Diane overlooked her mother's needs and adjustment to a new husband. Newlyweds strive to make a good impression and to please their companion. Diane's mother, Ginny, was caught between a rock and a hard place wanting to please her husband while being available for her children.

73

Whichever choice your newlywed parent makes will be the wrong choice either to you or to his or her spouse. Now is the time to recognize that Mom or Dad cannot please everyone, and more often than not you find yourself on the short end of the stick. A marital relationship should take precedence over the parent/child relationship. Extenuating circumstances would include major life changes such as a death, a marriage, serious health issues, or birth of a baby. Learn to appreciate new limitations on your parent's support and time. In working with newly formed stepfamilies in counseling, I have discovered that it is a two-step development process. First, you have to build the marriage. After some time, the marriage is strong enough to begin building new relationships with children.

Perhaps you can take on a new role and seize the opportunity to step up and support your newlywed parent. Several years into her mother's remarriage, Diane experienced an "aha" moment. She realized her behavior hurt rather than helped her mother. At the end of a visit, Diane's stepfather, Jim, was hospitalized in intensive care. Of course, Diane was at her mother's side offering whatever help was needed to her and Jim. Through her mother's actions rather than her words, Diane realized her mom's stress trying to balance marriage and motherhood desires. "I wanted to try harder to make things better for my mom. I saw that mom was obviously struggling too. My anger with Jim and not wanting a relationship with him was not helping my mom. She was doing the best she could. That situation made my relationship better with Jim because I was willing to try harder for my mom's sake."

Most parents and children are doing the best they can in any given situation, and all experience heartache when needs or desires are unfulfilled. In your new supporting role, be patient, especially during the first year while everyone is adapting. Talk to your mom or dad and ask if there is anything specific you can do to help. Bear in mind that your parent is part of a couple, and how you treat your stepparent affects your relationship with your parent. Make an effort to develop a relationship, as Trudie learned the hard way.

New Role as Stepchild

Trudie called her dad periodically after his wedding. "Every time I called, Helen answered the phone. I called to talk to my dad, not to Helen. Without trying to engage her in conversation, I asked to speak to my father. I felt like she was trying to show ownership of her new residence, my dad's house. Why would I want to talk to a relative stranger? In retrospect, I think it was her way of trying to initiate a relationship, and I completely brushed it aside. Several years passed before I tried to engage Helen in a phone conversation."

It seems as though Trudie forgot her manners. Common courtesy and civility are beneficial in everyday interactions. Trudie could have taken a few moments to ask her stepmother how she was doing or if anything of interest had happened since they last spoke. This simple gesture promotes goodwill and plants a seed for a relationship to grow.

Katie experienced a different dilemma during phone conversations. Her stepmother, Beverly, also answered the phone when Katie called. Katie made efforts to carry on a conversation with Beverly before speaking with her dad. Throughout Katie's conversation with her dad, Beverly listened on another extension. Beverly's behavior extended to visits as she followed Katie and her dad into the shop while they worked on a project. Katie described Beverly's personality as jealous and paranoid. "Beverly talks about us children behind our backs." She assumed Katie would do the same if she wasn't listening to conversations or present at all times during visits. Katie remained pleasant, cordial, and nonjudgmental of Beverly. After several years, Katie earned Beverly's trust and is now allowed private conversations and time with her dad.

Like Katie, you may have enjoyed a close relationship with your parents that included private time together doing hobbies and making projects. Your new stepparent may have different ideas of how your mom or dad should spend time with you or may be jealous of private time spent with you. Katie's behavior proved successful for her. She made several right choices that encouraged Beverly to replace jealousy and paranoia with trust and acceptance. She made the effort to talk to her stepmother; she accepted her stepmother's behavior as an outgrowth of her personality without judging or criticizing; she continued to seek her father's help and advice; she included Beverly in decisions regarding her dad's time.

Kristen's dad and stepmother lived in a different state with few relatives close by, so they had lots of time together to develop their relationship. Kristen continued to call regularly to check on them. Her friendship with Mary grew as they chatted on the phone. Kristen knew that in order to have a relationship with her dad she had to get along with her stepmother and wanted to make the effort.

As parents and children move further away from each other, visits become irregular. Phone contact is a common mode of maintaining relationships. Your stepmom's voice answering dad's phone may catch you off guard, but it is her phone now, too. Learn to go with the flow of changes and prepare yourself for the first visit home.

Visiting the Newlyweds

Your first visit to the newlyweds' residence will probably clarify the changes in your relationship. "There's no way to prepare yourself," said Melanie, remembering her first visit to her mom's new home. "That first visit was an eye opener. I heard noises in the bedroom!" She had to get used to the idea that she was no longer the focus of her mom's life. Subsequent visits were more comfortable, and Melanie adapted to the new normal.

Trudie's family planned an excursion near her dad's home. She called and asked if they could stop to visit. "I approached the door and wondered if I should knock or walk in as I had always done. I chose to knock and the rest of the visit was just as formal as we sat facing one another in the living room. I asked to use the restroom facilities and requested a drink of water. Since it was my former home, my actions felt foreign yet appropriate under the circumstances." Trudie said that subsequent visits have become less formal but still somewhat stilted.

Similarly, your comfortable relationship with your parent may feel stiff or unnatural until you adapt to the changes. Try to relax and just be yourself. This may be a long-term relationship, so let your best self shine through. Before long, you are once again comfortable.

What Do I Call My Stepparent?

Inwardly, you may bristle at using the term "stepfather" or "stepmother." This person has never been—and will never be—your parent in the traditional sense. He or she hasn't raised you, nurtured you, or disciplined you. "Stepparent" carries with it the implication of a "substitute parent," which as an adult you may neither want nor need. Similarly, your new stepparent isn't your peer either, so you may feel uncomfortable calling them by their first name, a practice that may connote too much familiarity for your tastes. Referring to a stepmother as "Mom" may feel unnatural. You already have a mother! Calling your stepfather "Mr. So-and-So" sounds much too formal and stilted in this day and age. But referring to him as "my mother's husband" is too convoluted and impersonal. In the worst-case scenario, you refrain from calling him anything, which grows ever more awkward as time goes by.

Sarah chose to call her stepparents by their given names. "At my age, I can't imagine calling a stepparent 'Mom' or 'Dad.' You have your parents whether they are dead or divorced," she said.

As contact increases and the relationship progresses with your stepparent, you may ease into calling them by more familiar terms. "My sisters and I have always been respectful of our stepmother," said Katie. "One sister even calls her 'Mom.' I call her Beverly." Katie's sister lives near their dad and Beverly; therefore, she has more interaction with them than the rest of the family. Calling Beverly "Mom" was a natural progression of their relationship.

Two of Neal's four children call Anne "Mom." "It was easy," said Anne. Amy wanted her children to call Anne "Grandma," because they no longer had a grandmother. "I was comfortable with that," said Anne. Amy and Anne's friendship since both were in high school facilitated broaching the subject, and they adapted easily to their new relationship.

Steve said, "I call my stepfather 'Nolan.' He's not my father and he won't replace my father. I don't feel comfortable calling him 'Dad.' I don't need another father. Calling Nolan 'Dad' would be phony and dishonest for me."

In the end, it's always safest to ask your stepparent if he or she has a preference. As long as it's respectful, courteous, and everyone's comfortable, you'll be okay. Use this advice for social introductions as well.

Make an Effort

Author and philosopher Thomas Moore writes about "welcoming the unfamiliar" in his book *Original Self: Living with Paradox and Authenticity*. "One concrete way to do this," he writes, "is to travel with an open mind, not judging others by what you already know and love." Now you have a stepparent who may be a virtual stranger to you. Communication may be awkward. How are you supposed to act around him or her? That depends largely on the relationship you have with your parent. Maybe your mother expects you to instantly embrace her new husband as one of the family, but you're having a hard time with that. You need to do something to bridge the gap between stranger and family. The best advice is to be yourself. Be gracious and welcoming. Open your arms and your home and invite your stepparent in. Don't be too anxious to promote the "way we've always done things."

Melanie's stepfather, Dan, was always warm and welcoming toward her, so it was natural for her to reciprocate. Dan sometimes visits Melanie's family by himself. "He feels comfortable with us and we appreciate his visits," Melanie said.

At least twice a week, Kristen talks with her stepmother, Mary. Through their joint efforts Kristen and Mary have developed a cherished friendship. Even if Mary weren't married to her father, said Kristen, "I would want to be her friend." They have developed a special and lasting bond.

Not everyone has the same easy transition. Emotions may get jarred as everyone feels as though they are trying hard to be accommodating but the result is that they still feel uncomfortable around each other. Trudie said her youngest brother was still living at home when their mother died. "When our dad got engaged, he told my brother he would have to move out. My brother was already devastated from our mother's sudden death. He felt like he was being kicked out of his home—all because of this woman who was about to move in. Everything our stepmother did was misjudged. His dislike of her was obvious and still is. I think our stepmother tried hard to be nice to him, but he was too hurt to accept it." If you are at fault, consider the ramifications of your behavior and determine if you want to continue in that direction. You can make a course correction at any time. If you feel your stepparent is at fault, don't try to force acceptance. Be cordial and make the effort to understand your stepparent's personality and the dynamics of the new relationships.

Sarah felt the awkwardness that existed between her and her stepfather for a long time, but after several years it finally dissipated. Sarah made the effort to engage him in conversation when she called, asking him about fishing expeditions or other trips before asking to speak to her mother. "It has opened up my heart toward him," Sarah reflected.

Marie noted that her daughter, Robin, rarely asks about her husband, John: "It's very difficult. It's heartbreaking. I almost feel like I'm living two separate lives. . . . When I visit Robin's family, they seldom, if ever, ask about John. . . . I think he would like to have a relationship. I don't think for a minute that my kids would do anything to hurt me. Yet it hurts me when they don't ask about John or even acknowledge the fact that I have a husband. It's like they are trying to shove him out of their lives and forget that he's there." Even though Marie recognizes the strained relations between Robin and John, she knows Robin loves her. Marie has not let the relationship between her husband and her daughter hamper her interactions. She visits her daughter and welcomes her to her home. She also appreciates the initiative of her other daughters who ask about John.

You no doubt appreciate the interest your stepparent shows in your children. When you appear indifferent to your stepparent or their family, you give the impression that you don't care. The simple act of asking after them helps dispel some of the awkwardness and is one way to bridge the chasm that is sometimes felt in new relationships. Most people like to talk about themselves, and even those who don't like to brag about their family! Express some interest and bridge an emotional chasm that will only grow wider if neglected.

Some people are blessed with the ability to converse easily and put others at ease. You may not have the gift now, but it's a skill that can be developed with practice. Start with a topic your stepparent knows well, a hobby, a book they're reading, or their family. It's a small effort that can reap huge rewards. As you learn more about your stepparent, your interest in them will increase, and you will be able to talk to them more easily. Keep in mind that your stepparent may feel just as awkward as you. After all, they're entering a family as a stranger. They, too, are sorting through new situations and emotions and trying to figure out their new role.

Trudie recognized a difference in the way her children related to her in-laws and to her father and his new wife: "My in-laws inquire about our children's welfare, activities, and interests. They talk with them on the phone and interact with them during visits," she said. "My dad and his wife ask how our children are doing and that's the end of that conversation.... I know my dad loves them, but he doesn't know how to interact with them. It's sad because he doesn't know them."

Anyone can improve his or her social interactions, including you. Determine what you can do to improve your relationship. Conscientiously practice the change asking trusted confidantes to help you. When you slip into your old habit, consider how you should have reacted and remember it for the next situation.

Should you reminisce about the absent parent in front of the new stepparent? That depends on your relationship and everyone's comfort level. "Within months of my dad's remarriage we had an extended-family birthday party for him," said Trudie. "Our mother hadn't been dead even a year and it was the first time we had been together after the wedding. It was natural for us to reminisce about our mother. We shared stories and memories. Helen was very quiet and sat with her head somewhat bowed. It was apparent that she was feeling uncomfortable. I tried to be more careful after that." Be sensitive to the fact that talking about your absent parent in front of your new stepparent could give the impression that you are drawing comparisons. There's nothing wrong with sharing memories, and some stepparents may want to participate. Use your best judgment. If necessary, reminisce privately with your parent or siblings.

Do Things Together

For some people, doing is easier than talking. One of the great things about participating in various activities is that the talk often flows naturally from the interaction. Nicole took her son fishing whenever she had something she wanted to teach him. As he matured and wanted his mother's advice, he asked, "Mother, can we go fishing?"

Steve appreciates his stepfather's participation in various family activities. "Nolan has done things that have been beneficial in the relationship to build trust and good feelings, like gift giving, friendliness, showing up with my mom at grandchildren's events. He's gone on trips and participated in activities like snorkeling with the younger people, in a way that I don't even know if my dad could have. He has a playful way about him. He's willing to jump into whatever activity is going on. That is his nature." During such activities you may begin by discussing the activity, and your conversation soon evolves to include other topics of interest or concern. It's one way to strengthen relationships in a mature stepfamily and to adjust to the new family dynamic.

Many families have hobbies, sports, and activities that they have shared over many years. For some it's the touch football games after Thanksgiving dinner; for others, it's singing or playing instruments. It could even be creating family scrapbooks of photos and memories, building models, fishing, or putting jigsaw puzzles together. Ruth said, "Music has always been a big part of my life as my family sang, and now my children carry on the tradition." Ruth's husband, Dave, was a high school band teacher. When they married, music remained a vital part of family activities. Ruth said, "We have a lot of music. We sing while someone plays the piano or guitar. Even Janice, who has developmental disabilities, joins in. Everyone participates in one way or another." They value the joy, entertainment, and unity that music has brought to their family.

A **Stepparent's** Perspective

Time spent engaging in activities helped Marie and her children and stepchildren adapt to their new roles. "When you marry, you marry the family," said Marie. "This wasn't as clear to my husband when we married. . . . When they come to visit, I spend the whole time with the grandchildren or his daughter or daughter-in-law. John will say, 'Here's some money. Why don't you take them out to the movies?' Then he disappears. . . . I've done things such as reupholstering my stepdaughter's chairs for her—and consequently, we have a wonderful relationship." As Marie knows, it's the personal attention and the conversations that build enduring relationships.

Music connects family generations. You may not especially like the "oldie goldies" of your parents' generation (or they yours!), but you should be able to find some musical common ground. Whether your musical talents are good, bad, or so-so, singing and playing together is one way to draw your family closer. Singing or playing instruments together is a collective invitation to all to participate. Everyone can join in the merrymaking regardless of ability. Joy in singing not only blends voices but it also blends hearts.

Games, sports, movies, or outdoor activities promote frivolity and encourage participation and lightheartedness by relaxing and enjoying togetherness. These leisure activities also teach trust and respect for others through cooperative efforts. You may discover a latent talent or a common interest with your stepparent. Katie grew up playing games with her family. The tradition continues, "When we get together, we play games. We just hang out. I don't think that's changed that much when my dad and stepmother married." A favorite pastime is a natural way to include your stepparent in the family circle.

What if someone doesn't want to participate? Meg and Ken offer a solution: "We play games with some members of both sides of the family. Each of us has one or two spoil sports who make comments like, 'If you start playing games, I'm leaving.' That is their problem and there is little we can do about a negative attitude," Meg said. They continue to play games without letting the one or two spoil the fun.

Recreational activities provide entertainment, relaxation, exercise, and companionship. They are usually a nonthreatening way to interact and knit hearts together as you help and cheer one another or work as a team. You may not remember specific conversations during outings or activities, but the fun times playing together are indelibly etched in your memory. There's no reason why you can't continue these activities—the raw material out of which family memories are created—and invite your stepparent to participate.

Trudie recalled a family barbecue during which they played croquet: "I don't remember if my dad and stepmother actually played, but they were there talking and laughing with us as we told stories and teased one another while awaiting our turn. The lightheartedness of the day is what I remember most connecting three generations."

Play could take the form of a hobby. Hobbies provide a mental escape from everyday pressures while still engaging our minds and bodies. Katie's dad taught his children to work with wood, and she appreciates her dad's time and expertise. "I like to build things with my dad," Katie said. "We built my cupboards and he cut them out. Dad takes great pride in helping us."

A **Parent's** Perspective

Some couples prefer to do everything together. Nick said of his marriage to Mary, "We're a happy couple. We do everything together. And it couldn't be better." Knowing this about her father and stepmother, Kristen accepts the fact that her dad and Mary prefer doing everything together, and she accommodates their desire by inviting them to join her family for dinner or go out with her and her husband.

All parents are proud to watch their children develop as they discover and use their talents. As a child yourself, you can appreciate the time and attention your parents gave you. Parents are pleased to see you continue activities that have always been important to your family. They like to offer advice and share their knowledge. Stepparents are no different. They want to feel they are contributing, needed, and useful. It's a familiar role that you can share.

Building Relationships Despite Distance or Large Families

If you live near your stepparent, it will of course be easier to spend time together and ease into the family changes. Richard lived 600 miles away from his father and stepmother, Nancy, when they married. His father does more with Nancy's children and their families, who live in the same city, than he does with Richard's family. Consequently, the adjustment has been easier on Nancy's family. After moving across the country,

Richard's dad and stepmother visited his family. They went sightseeing, toured historical sites, and did other activities with his family. Richard's wife said it gave her an opportunity to talk with Nancy and discuss issues of concern. Heartfelt conversations cleared up some worries.

Distance apart is one challenge that makes regular family interaction more difficult. Often the size of the combined family is another. Recognize that your parent and stepparent may not have the funds to acknowledge every birthday or attend every event, but appreciate every effort they make. Sandy knows that her mother and stepfather's attendance at parties and events is the greatest support she can receive from them. "Mom and Dean have over a hundred grandchildren together. As far as gifts and cards, they don't have the money. But they always attend events whenever there's a birthday, baby blessing, or baptism."

Show Your Stepparent How You Feel

George Sand wrote, "There is only one happiness in life, to love and be loved." When someone offers you love, you feel secure, warm, and content. It's an indescribable yet recognizable sensation. Love is the greatest gift you can give to your parent and stepparent when it's freely given and heartfelt. One way to show your love is to make an effort to find ways to spend time together. It will nurture your love and help you to feel secure and content.

"Love" and "family" imply sacrifice. Freely giving your time, energy, or other resources for the well-being of your family demonstrates your love, offers a sense of security, and brings you contentment. Parents willingly make sacrifices for their children, from saving for college instead of installing a new bathroom, to working long hours to provide music lessons or pay for family vacations. Sometimes a parent's remarriage can turn his or her attention away from you. Their gifts of time, financial aid, or emotional support may diminish as they spend more time with the new spouse. Sometimes we only notice—and appreciate—something when it's no longer there.

A **Parent's** Perspective

Some parents don't recognize their service as sacrifice since it is a natural outgrowth of their love for you. Nick said, "I haven't made any sacrifices for my family." Mary reminded him that they attend birthdays, activities, and religious events; and they fly to various states to visit their children. Those are sacrifices freely given and should be graciously accepted. Nick and Mary were quick to acknowledge their children's efforts to go out of their way to spend time with them. Be appreciative of what they do for you.

Sarah had two small boys and had just given birth to twins when her father married Lois. She needed and longed for their support. "It would have meant so much to me if they had said, 'Could we take the kids for a couple of hours?'" The situation further strained their tenuous relationship.

Asking for Help

Of course, you appreciate any sacrifice your parent or stepparent makes, but you may be reluctant to ask for help. Sometimes the simple act of asking and receiving help smoothes the adjustments in the changing family relationship. Helping one another is something people in families do, and happily, because you want to show your love.

"What has worked really well for my sister," said Steve, "is to ask Nolan to do things for her. He picks up children from school when everybody's in a bind, which he is willing to do. People haven't learned very well to ask for help. One of the best things you can do if you want to develop a relationship with someone is to ask that person to do something for you. Asking sort of opens the way, helping the stepparent to fit."

You may be reluctant to ask for help, but what's the worst thing that could happen? You could be turned down. That's when you look for another avenue. Chances are your parent and stepparent will be glad you asked and happy to do what they can.

Richard appreciates the financial and emotional support of his father and stepmother. "I feel that if we were in a jam, Dad and Nancy would step in and help do whatever we needed help with," he said.

Sandy also recognizes the sacrifices her stepfather makes for her mother and family, "Dean knew how much my mother loved being close to family and friends," she said. "He wouldn't make her move. He had a home in another city, which he sold, and he moved into my mother's home. He made that sacrifice for Mom." Sandy continued, "Dean's support has meant everything. He is an important part of our family because he is always there for us, and that means a lot."

Sandy can see how much Dean loves her, her mother, and her family. Sandy experiences a fatherly relationship with Dean that she didn't have with her own father. Dean's sacrifices helped her adapt to the changes in her old role and embrace her new role.

Identity Versus Role Confusion

This phase of your relationship deviates from Erikson's progressive order of development, mentioned in an earlier chapter. Like the teenager trying to discover his talents and interests to determine who he is and what he wants to do the rest of his life, you are trying to figure out your role with your stepparent, understand the changes in the relationship with your parent, and discern your place in this new marriage. You may feel confused at times with the evolving roles. Even as teenagers sometimes experiment with delinquent behavior or rebellion, you may hear yourself saying or see yourself doing things potentially offensive or out of line. The successful adolescent develops a set of ideals that help him achieve his potential. You, too, can develop a set of ideals to help you realize your desired relationships. You rediscover who you really are by exercising self-control in your behavior. In the process, your role in new and familiar relationships emerges. You once again learn who you are and how you fit in.

The key here is to be proactive rather than reactive in defining your new roles. Decide what kind of positive person you want to be in these new relationships. Visualize how your behavior would look as you become that person, and give it a try. If your parent or new stepparent doesn't behave in exactly the ways you anticipated, don't be emotionally reactive, but continue to behave congruent with the positive role you are defining for yourself.

Take Action

If you have a relationship akin to Trudie's brother where you are judgmental or critical and you want to change, first of all, you are probably being reactive rather than taking charge of your own behavior. In his book, *The Seven Principles for Making Marriage Work,* psychologist John Gottman reports that the ratio of positive comments to criticism in successful relationships is 5 to 1. This positive comment tactic strengthens other relationships as well. You will need to work at increasing your compliments of your parent and new stepparent. In order to do this, you will have to watch carefully to find positive things to praise. Fight the temptation to focus on the negative behaviors, because that will only make you more unhappy. Determine that when you slip up and voice criticism about your parent and stepparent to anyone that you will apologize quickly and visualize how you will behave differently the next time.

If your stepparent is not responsive to your behavior, be patient. Try to understand his or her point of view and work at developing a relationship. In time it will most likely change. If it persists, schedule a time to talk to both your parent and stepparent and express what you want your relationship with both of them to be rather than criticizing or blaming. If it still doesn't change, you could ask if they would be willing to go with you to family counseling for a few sessions. If they refuse, then you will have to accept the situation, but you can still be in control of how you behave. The worst thing you can do is to avoid them.

Possible Scenario

The following is an example of a telephone conversation in which the child makes an effort to get to know her stepfather. One question leads to the next.

Child: Hi John. How are you today?

Stepparent: I'm doing okay.

Child: How was your fishing trip with your buddies?

Stepparent: We caught a few despite the poor conditions. My largest was a four-pounder that I caught with a fly my buddy let me try.

Child: Where do you usually fish and how long were you gone?

Stepparent: We fish on the Snake River and spend a couple of days.

Child: Is my mom there, so I can talk to her now?

Stepparent: She's not here now. But I'll tell her you called.

The conversation need not be long, but it shows an interest in the other individual and represents your effort to develop a relationship.

The Heart of the Matter

H.R.H. Prince Phillip said, "Change is a challenge and an opportunity, not a threat." As your role in the family changes, you may experience some anxiety. Your ability to adapt with good humor and grace will go a long way toward maintaining a loving relationship with your new stepparent. These simple pointers will help smooth your way.

- Ask directly how your stepparent would like to be addressed. Show respect and make sure both of you are comfortable with it.
- Treat your stepparent just as you would like to be treated. The Golden Rule isn't just for little kids.
- Engage your stepparent in conversation to get better acquainted. Ask questions. Learn about her or his interests and talents and inquire about family. Ask your parent for suggestions if you feel unsure about what to ask. Initiating conversations shows your interest in your stepparent and that you want to be friends. You might consider inviting your stepparent of the same gender to lunch, just the two of you.
- Spend one-on-one time with your parent. This helps you to adjust to changes in your familiar role as his or her child. Initiate the visits yourself if you have to. Respect

your parent's desire to have his or her spouse there during the visit.

- Enjoy family activities with your stepparent and parent. Invite her or him to soccer games, recitals, birthday parties, and other events. Engage in projects or take trips together to draw your family closer together. Adjust your activities to fit the circumstances. If a parent or stepparent can't participate in an activity for reasons of age, health, or proximity, find other ways to communicate together, such as instant messaging, e-mails, phone calls, or the old-fashioned letter.

- Recognize and appreciate the sacrifices your parent and stepparent make on your behalf. They may not be aware of your needs unless you let them know how and when you need help. Look for ways to reciprocate.

CHAPTER 6

"You Like Your Stepchildren
Better Than Me!"

"When you're part of a team, you stand up for your teammates. Your loyalty is to them. You protect them through good and bad, because they'd do the same for you."

—*Yogi Berra*

Dad has always been one of your best buds. You may have fond memories of attending baseball games together, changing the oil in the car, early-morning hikes, or late-night heart-to-heart talks. Then there's Mom—your secret keeper, your shopping partner, your cooking mentor, and your chauffeur for lessons and practices. You could always count on Mom and Dad for their unconditional love—your loyal fans, always available to listen, give advice, or cheer you on in your endeavors.

You never dreamed that one day Dad would say, "Now isn't a good time to visit." Or that Mom would say, "I'm sorry, honey, I can't help you out today." What happened to their unconditional love? Are their stepchildren more important to them than I am? So much for family unity! All you needed was a babysitter for an hour. What will happen when you have a real emergency? Will Mom or Dad be available to help? The intimacy you once felt with your mom or dad may give way to feelings of isolation.

Perhaps you are more fortunate than those struggling with loyalty conflicts. You have a great relationship with your mom or dad and like your new stepparent. You've adjusted well to your new role as stepchild. Now it's time to get used to your new extended family and figure out stepsibling relationships.

Loyalty Conflicts

Loyalty issues are always involved in remarriage and the formation of a new stepfamily. Loyalty is an inherently felt belonging and advocacy to a parent, especially in the case of a deceased parent. Accepting a new stepparent and awareness of affection and intimacy in the new marriage of your parent often brings out intense advocacy, like, I need to carry the torch for my deceased mother who is not here. Adult children often guard against liking a new stepparent because they feel they are being disloyal to their biological mom or dad who is deceased. This is a challenge that requires effort to change.

Loyalty and the Death of a Parent

Following the death of a parent, divided loyalties are usually not a problem unless Mom or Dad remarries too quickly for your liking or his or her spouse forces your parent to take sides. Fierce loyalty to your deceased parent may surface, stifling your ability to support Mom or Dad—let alone desire a relationship with your new stepparent.

For example, Patricia's cousins were obviously upset when their dad married within a year of their mother's sudden death. "Their mother was an awesome woman. My Uncle Jack's children were furious that he remarried so quickly. His children were awful to Faye. Faye drove a wedge in their relationship with their dad. It's worked well for Faye because Jack is close to her children. Faye insisted that Jack back her up on everything. Jack did until he had no relationship with his children. Jack's children have absolutely nothing to do with their dad and his wife. Jack does not even know where his children live."

This example illustrates how divided loyalties can literally destroy family relationships. With the death of their mother still poignantly smarting, Jack's children were unable to see past their pain to sympathize with their dad's desire to remarry. Faye's reciprocal rude behavior further fueled their bitterness. Jack's children and his wife had expectations of him. Unfortunately, the expectations were contradictory rather than complementary. Jack had to choose. He took sides, standing behind his wife and giving her his loyalty and support. As Jack sided with his wife, his children probably felt him pulling away from them. Jack sacrificed his children for his wife. It is easy to comprehend why children in a similar situation would feel abandoned, having lost a mother to death and lost Dad's loyalty to another family.

Consider the other side of the story. Jack's children also made choices. Their choices and resultant behavior demonstrated their loyalty to their mother at the expense of their relationship with their father. In essence, they also forced their father to take sides, perhaps expecting him to love them and do right by them regardless of their behavior. If you can relate to Jack's children, you may experience feelings of betrayal. Betrayal is felt when, in your eyes, your living parent betrays your deceased parent by marrying too quickly, when he or she sides with a stepparent rather than with you, and when you forsake your living parent on behalf of your deceased parent. This web of betrayal quickly becomes very complicated and complex. In his article "Divided Loyalties: The Challenge of Stepfamily Life" published in the *Family Therapy Networker*,

Dr. William J. Doherty says, "For children, the challenge is to find a way to honor the stepparent without dishonoring the original parent."

Let's examine another instance where children felt betrayed. Diane's mother was on a trip with her husband, Jim, when Diane's sister-in-law died unexpectedly soon after childbirth. Diane's mother, Ginny, and Jim stopped at her son's home on their return flight to see the new baby, unaware of the tragedy. Diane expected her mother to stay and help her brother and his four children. Instead, Ginny and Jim returned to their house to prepare for an upcoming cruise. Ginny told Diane, "For the sake of my marriage, I just can't stay." Diane was shocked: "That was hurtful to me and the rest of my siblings." Diane felt that if anything happened to her husband or her family, she could not count on her mother to be there. Eventually, Ginny tried to make amends by returning off and on for about six months to help her son and grandchildren. An interesting thing about trust and loyalty is that once violated, they are not easily regained. No matter how hard an individual tries to earn lost loyalty, previous experience causes doubt to remain.

Diane knew that her mother would have felt no qualms of leaving her father to care for their son and grandchildren, and her dad would have accepted it, since his wife would be attending to family needs. The needs of father-mother-son would have balanced, forming an equilateral triangle of family support. However, in reality, the triangle of stepfather-mother-son was unbalanced with no one's needs fully met. The son lacked the immediate support of his mother. Ginny felt pressured to accompany her husband, and then tried to overcome feelings of guilt by returning to help her son. Jim eventually conceded and allowed Ginny time with her family. Finding that fine balance is difficult especially when one or the other, spouse or child, demands complete loyalty. Another challenge of children then is to understand and accept what time and support your parent is able and willing to give under the circumstances.

Nicole's family represents a third example of loyalty conflicts. After Nicole's father died, her mother, Esther, married a widower who wanted little to do with either family. Nicole's mother had always supported and helped her children and welcomed them in her home when they visited from out of town. After her marriage, Esther permitted her children to stay in her vacant house but had reduced interaction with them and was unavailable to help them and grandchildren. Nicole and her siblings kept in touch with their mother and became more and more uncomfortable with her marital situation. After more than twenty years, Esther divorced her husband. Her children supported her decision, and one even provided her a place to live.

At first glance, you may wonder if any loyalties exist in this example. The husband seems self-absorbed in isolating himself and Esther from their children. Esther seems to be half-heartedly complying with her husband. However, the children remain loyal to their mother, welcoming her home with open arms after she recognizes the folly of her decision. When a marriage ends in divorce, loyalties generally revert to family ties.

Loyalty and Divorce

With divorce, some parents attempt to win their children's loyalties. They compete for your love as though relationships are competitions with winners and losers. You're standing on the sidelines supporting them both. Perhaps one parent no longer merits your trust, and you naturally gravitate toward the deserving parent. Yet because of your love for the undeserving parent, you may long for a relationship. Add a stepparent to the mix and loyalties can really become unbalanced. If you experienced guilt for overt loyalty to one parent, you may feel justified after your other parent's new marriage. If you remain neutral, you stand a better chance of preserving relationships with both parents.

Sarah's parents divorced when she was a young mother. She continued to love both parents. Her parents lived in another country, and Sarah's dad even met his second wife while visiting Sarah's family. The alienation she felt when her family was excluded from the wedding party continued throughout the duration of the marriage. Sarah's stepmother, Lois, focused on her children, doting on them and her grandchildren. Occasionally, Sarah's dad and Lois accepted an invitation to join Sarah's family for an activity, but Sarah could sense their anxiousness to leave.

Sarah's stepmother exhibited unfairness beginning with the wedding and continuing on from there by giving preferential treatment to her children. Her father's loyalty to his wife and her children induced feelings of betrayal and abandonment. Sarah felt little if any altruism from her stepmother.

Accept the Challenge

The challenge is to honor your stepparent without dishonoring your parent—but that might make you feel like you are being disloyal to a deceased parent. In reality, however, honoring one may in fact be honoring the other, and dishonoring one may dishonor the other. Closer scrutiny brings this issue into clearer focus and may present solutions, much like a microscope enables the researcher to find answers to her queries. If your parents had a good marriage, chances are your deceased parent would want the surviving spouse to be happy and to enjoy a good quality of life, which marriage usually offers. Your deceased parent would want you to be supportive of the marriage and your new stepparent. Therefore, to honor your parent's memory you will want to honor your stepparent.

How do you do that? Consider the teachings of your parents. Most parents teach their children to honor others by being kind. That includes being courteous, respecting your elders, and being nonjudgmental and complimentary rather than critical. These behaviors infuse your relationships with fairness, loyalty, and altruism. Isn't that what you would want from your stepparent?

Courtesy and Cordiality

*"The nearer you come into relation with a person, the more
necessary do tact and courtesy become. Except in cases of
necessity, which are rare, leave your friend to learn unpleasant
things from his enemies; they are ready enough to tell them."*
—*Oliver Wendell Holmes*

Courtesy toward and consideration of a stepparent, or lack thereof, affects you and your stepparent. Courtesy fosters friendship by making life pleasant and encourages you to spend time together. It inspires a personal regard for each other. Courtesy guards against the buffetings of misunderstanding, mistrust, and hostility. We've already seen how reciprocal rude behavior destroyed Jack's family relationships. Now let's see the outcome of consideration for others.

Earlier, we met Patricia, whose cousins called their stepmother blessed. Her uncle Calvin had married Audrey, whose loving consideration for the children and Calvin won their loyalty: "Heartbroken and still grieving their mother's death, Calvin's children were rude to their new stepmother. When the children said something mean or did something awful, Audrey never took it personally. She always let it slide; she was not hurt or upset. Audrey never complained to her husband. She overlooked every rotten thing the children did and never

99

discussed it with their father. Audrey understood and expected Calvin's children would be upset. She never stressed over it. She let them rage, being rude and disrespectful. Audrey just said, 'They'll be okay.' When the time was right, Audrey was there to embrace those children.

"It took a couple of years for the children to calm down. Because Audrey never struck out or back at them, the door was totally open for a relationship. After a couple of years, the children started noticing a good thing here and there about Audrey. She didn't hold anything against them. Audrey didn't judge them. Every one of Calvin's six children loves her and appreciates her. She's a good woman." Audrey is an amazing example of patience, serenity, and courtesy. She took the high road and it paid off.

Of course, children grieve following a parent's death. You can't put a timeline on grief. Your parent's remarriage may intensify your grieving, causing bitterness and anger. Who better to direct those emotions toward than your stepparent? If it weren't for him or her, you would have more of your parent's attention. Audrey understood those feelings in her stepchildren. She was patient while they worked through their grieving and could eventually accept her love.

A Stepparent's Questionable Behavior

Children aren't the only ones who are rude and inconsiderate. Some stepparents forget the manners they taught their offspring. They may be blind to the effects of their behavior. Rude behavior begins to decay relationships, and sometimes rude behavior becomes such a problem that stepchildren no longer communicate with their stepparents. Can it be reversed? The answer is a resounding "yes" and requires an unrelenting exercise of courtesy, as Audrey experienced. Responsibility to try to reverse the direction of the relationships falls upon you, the stepchild. Immunize yourself against unkindness by remaining committed to courtesy as Audrey did. With vigilant kindness, you also can effectuate a change of heart in your stepparent. In the meantime, how should you react to potentially offensive behavior?

- You may ask, "What if my stepfather ignores me?"
  Be courteous and always acknowledge him.
- "What if my stepmother listens to phone conversations with dad?"
  Accept it until she comes to trust you.
- "What if they offend me?"
  Be courteous and overlook it or be quick to forgive.

Suspicion, animosity, or other negative emotions cloud your thinking and may lead to impolite actions. Love and kindness can overcome negative emotions and outcomes. Your relationship with your parent also requires consideration, especially of his or her right to make decisions. It does not mean that you agree with every choice. You can politely and tactfully express your opinions, then assure Mom or Dad of your love with a continued outpouring of kindness.

A **Stepparent's** Perspective

Dave described how mutual courtesy with Ruth's children facilitated their friendship: "I guess the way I interacted must be a good way because I never had any problems with Ruth's children. It was just like I'd always been here. You just be yourself and be nice, and by golly they're nice back to you!" The kindness of Ruth's children helped Dave to feel part of the family when he and Ruth married. Kindness begat kindness. Courtesy worked for Dave and Ruth, as it has worked for many others throughout time.

Gracious and courteous behavior has the power to overcome offensiveness and to develop cherished friendships. Recall Audrey's example at the beginning of this section when she drew the hearts of her stepchildren toward her. Courtesy and consideration empower you to persevere when confronted with unkindness and at the same time nurture love and acceptance in your stepparent.

Respect

"To have respect for ourselves guides our morals; and to have a deference for others governs our manners."
—*Lawrence Sterne*

Respect for your parent and stepparent represents loyalty and further fortifies friendship. Respect manifests itself through a sincere concern for the well-being of those whom you love most. Gracious verbal and nonverbal interactions characterize respect. Thinking more of the needs of others and less of your own shows respect, decreases selfishness, and increases happiness. Deference given to a stepparent naturally flows back to you. Writing for *Psychology Today*, Virginia Rutter said, "Parents must require kids and stepparents to treat one another with respect. Only then can bonds between them develop."

A **Parent's** Perspective
Speaking of respect Neal said, "Anne's children have to respect me, and my kids have to respect her. Neither one of us will let anyone mistreat the other or talk bad about the other. I think it is important to teach respect, and you have to earn respect. Parents can't assume that these new relationships will work; they won't work if we're not respected by our children."

In successful marriages and families, husbands and wives respect each other and their children. Parents who model respect usually earn the esteem of their children. So, how do you earn the respect of your stepparent and vice versa? Honoring invisible boundaries is one way to earn respect.

Kristen shared the following story in which her stepmother, Mary, earned her respect, "When we were closing my parents' house, Mary was here helping my dad. While sorting my mother's personal belongings in the dresser, a drawer fell and Mary quickly said, 'Oh let me take care of that.' Realizing that she was overstepping her boundaries, Mary said, 'What would you like me to do?' That little incident told a whole lot about her and made us even more respectful of Mary." Accepting her position as a bit of an outsider in sorting her predecessor's personal belongings, Mary respected her stepchildren's desire to distribute their mother's possessions. Mary wanted her new family to know of her interest to help without crossing the boundary of privacy. She modeled respect for the family's feelings as well as their ability to handle their mother's personal items. She assisted without assuming authority to make decisions and earned the esteem of her stepchildren. As their mutual respect increased, Kristen and Mary's friendship evolved, enhanced by a growing loyalty.

Respecting Your Stepparent

It is important to treat your stepparent with respect, especially when he or she is in a sticky situation, such as sorting through a deceased spouse's belongings. To be respectful you don't have to understand how a stepparent feels or why he or she does something in a particular way or behaves in a certain manner. Esteeming your stepparent includes accepting without criticizing, being sincere without prying, and being serviceable without being overbearing. Mutual deference usually leads to enhanced understanding of each other's feelings.

Honoring feelings is another way to earn respect. Kristen continued, "I enjoy making wreaths for my mom's grave. While trying to get a wreath together and doing eight million things, Mary offers to reduce my stress by picking up flowers for me. I appreciate her offer and let her know it's something that I want to do for my mother. Mary totally understands. She's very respectful of my feelings."

Mary was sincere in her desire to help but did not force her services. She accepted Kristen's decision without being offended. Mary's respect of Kristen's feelings and her acceptance of her mother increased Kristen's esteem for her. Kristen appreciated Mary's efforts to honor her mother without trying to replace her. When individuals discipline themselves to respect the feelings of others, they create an environment that breeds mutual regard and inspires loyalty. In your effort to develop a friendship with your stepparent, respect his or her feelings and decisions.

Be Inclusive

"Let no one ever come to you without leaving better and happier. Be the living expression of God's kindness: kindness in your face, kindness in your eyes, kindness in your smile."
—*Mother Teresa*

Recall the feelings of alienation experienced by children who were excluded from their parent's wedding party and from family pictures. Exclusion causes isolation, quite the opposite of intimacy, which most people desire. Including your parent and stepparent in your family life is an easy way to develop intimacy or enduring friendships. It is another way to express your loyalty to Mom or Dad.

In the Eisenberger study on social exclusion cited previously, she and her colleagues determined that exclusion can come in two forms:

Explicit inclusion: when individuals are prevented by others from participating in an activity

Implicit exclusion: when individuals are not able to join in an activity because of extenuating circumstances

Behavior free of bias is equally important for you and your stepparent. From the onset of Neal and Anne's marriage, Neal's daughter, Amy, invited Anne and her children to parties. Anne said, "Amy has an Easter party and other functions for which we get together. When one of her kids is in town, Amy plans a party and invites her sisters and brother and always includes my children too. Amy refers to my children as her brother and sisters." Anne appreciated Amy's efforts to include her children in the family circle. Amy fostered friendships and built loyalty by treating both families equally.

Ruth's children included Dave in all their celebrations. Dave said, "There was no stuffiness. It's like we'd been friends forever. They made it easy on me by including me first. When Ruth and I married, it seemed like I was moving where I belonged. I liked and loved Ruth's children, and they reciprocated." One of Ruth's daughters said, "Dave has been a blessing to everyone in our family." Once again inclusion avoided offense, promoted fairness, and built loving friendships.

Trudie felt a definite bias against her when her dad sent a letter mentioning two family dinners at his home: "One was for his wife's children and the other for my two brothers. I live close enough that I could have attended but I wasn't invited." Using the pain as a catalyst, Trudie withdrew to protect herself from further pain.

The pain of exclusion is real and may cause an individual to withdraw emotionally from the relationship to guard against further pain. Rather than relieving the pain, retreating may have the opposite effect and cause additional pain. The pain persists until someone makes the effort of inviting family members into their life. Stepfamily relationships deteriorate when no one tries to improve them. If you are the excluded family member, you may continue to experience pain until Mom or Dad invites you to family activities or you make the effort.

Inclusive behavior strengthens relationships. Melanie lived with her mother when she started dating Dan. Melanie felt immediately accepted by Dan and explained why: "Dan's personality is very welcoming. He has a vivacious character about him. Dan is a Toastmaster, sings barbershop, and calls square dances. He is smart, personable, and charming. I've always felt welcome by him." Melanie naturally wanted to reciprocate by welcoming Dan into her life.

Some families are large and spread out, which makes it difficult to have everyone together at the same time and place. Sandy's mom and stepfather had a few summer parties together with both families. Because of the large number, combined activities didn't work that well. They now hold separate family parties. Sandy appreciates the efforts her mother and Dean made to include both families, and she understands their decision to have smaller gatherings. Separate but equal maintains fairness in stepfamilies as long as you feel no favoritism.

Withhold Judgment

"Our judgments judge us; and nothing reveals us [or] exposes our weaknesses more ingeniously than the attitude of pronouncing upon our fellows."
—Paul Valery

Our legal system espouses the theory of innocent until proven guilty. As citizens, we accept that as a constitutional right. Yet as individuals, we make judgments frequently before knowing all the facts. Sometimes our presumptions are false and hinder our relationships before they can take root. This issue of fairness affects loyalty, causing imbalance in the parent/stepparent/child relationship.

For example, Shirley's two stepdaughters assumed she was marrying their dad for his money and appeared to be overly concerned about expenditures and personal possessions. Shirley's daughter-in-law, Melanie, said, "Shirley finally had to sit down with her stepdaughters and explain how much she and their dad contributed for purchases and that expenses for vacations with Shirley's children came out of her personal funds. My mother-in-law probably has more money than her husband." The stepdaughters' false assumption prevented them from accepting Shirley.

Many are guilty at times of prejudging others before any or all the evidence is collected. Sadly, this occurs with stepfamilies when they base verdicts on hearsay, emotional reactions, or other subjective information resulting in an unjust verdict. Judging a new stepparent harshly before becoming acquainted is unkind, hampers the possibility of friendship, and infests your mind with faulty, preconceived notions. Some of the reasons for faulty judgments include misinterpreting behavior, misunderstanding role definitions, judging without understanding, inaccurate initial impressions, and unknown experiences.

In many cases you reach a different conclusion when you wait to know your stepparent before passing judgment. Withholding judgment until you understand facts and personalities leads to a fair verdict and enables you to keep an open mind about your stepparent and his or her relationship with your parent. You have time to collect and process information by observing behaviors and evolving relationships before judging. Being nonjudgmental eases the way for creating a foothold for loyalty.

Misunderstandings and Disagreements

When you are not familiar with someone's personality, there is always the chance that behaviors will be misinterpreted. For example, Marie's husband, John, tried to develop a relationship with stepfamily members through monetary means. Those who do not recognize monetary tokens as love might interpret John's behavior as aloof and uncaring. Marie explained, "My husband shows his love and affection by buying something for the kids and the same is true with me to a certain extent. Yet when the two of us are on our own, John is considerate and loving, almost like a different person." Marie's children only see John's behavior with them and could judge him as uninterested in them.

When an unjust verdict occurs, your parent, acting as a judge, can interpret your stepparent's behavior and thus dispel misperception. Your parent may also shed light on your stepparent's private behavior, thereby further dismissing inaccurate judgments.

Marie's husband and daughter, Janie, misjudged each other, causing friction. Marie helped them discuss the problem and facilitated a solution: "Janie was serving a religious mission in another country when John and I married. Janie and John didn't see eye-to-eye when they met. Years later they had this big blowout and from then on things were fine," Marie said.

Blowups occur in relationships when the pressure is too great to contain. It is like opening a soda can after shaking it—it bursts everywhere, fizzles, and calms down. People sometimes burst when pressure increases from holding feelings inside too long. After the initial burst, they calm down and things are once again fine. Janie was unaware of the turmoil brewing inside John every time she and her husband visited with their dog. Marie explained, "Janie and her husband had this big black dog that they brought to our home. John is very meticulous and would explode when the dog ran through his freshly planted garden. Finally, John and Janie had this big blowup over this issue. I said, 'Okay, enough! Both of you in the living room. Sit down. Let's get this straightened out once and for all.' We all decided that the best solution was that the dog not come with them any more when they came to visit. From then on their relationship just got better and better. But somebody finally had to say, 'Hey!'" Marie had had enough! Acting as judge, she sat the defendants down. They discussed the problem. Janie and John understood the other's perspective and feelings, and they reached a mutual agreement for solving the problem—leave the dog at home. Their feelings healed as they mended their relationship, which has continued to improve. Marie added, "John thinks the world of Janie and adores her children." Disagreements can be resolved and relationships can do an about face when misunderstandings and misjudgments are resolved.

First, recognize a problem exists. The second step is getting the involved parties to sit down and discuss the problem. Third, correctly understand the problem and each other's feelings. The fourth step is finding an acceptable solution and implementing it. A nonpartial judge, such as a family member, a professional marriage and family therapist, or religious leader, may facilitate the process. The well-known family therapist Virginia Satir stated in her book, *The New Peoplemaking*, that one of the marks of a successful family is being able to solve problems. When all family members have the goal of caring for each other, they can learn a set of problem-solving skills that will give them the confidence to work together. The key is to describe the problem in nonaccusatory language, avoid personal attacks, and regulate emotional reactivity. If that cannot be done, that presents a need for the involvement of an objective third party.

Lack of experience also causes misjudgment. Many times you cannot understand a stepparent's feelings unless you have experienced a similar situation. You base your verdict on known facts, disregarding the unknown. Until you know your stepparent's experiences and feelings, you may dismiss them as irrelevant. It is terrible, yet it happens. Emotions affect behavior, so some knowledge of your stepparent's feelings is important evidence in reaching an accurate verdict.

Sandy counsels, "refrain from judging right from the beginning. My sister-in-law lost her mother and her father remarried. My sister-in-law told me, 'I feel like I've lost my dad now since he married this woman, and she's all he cares about.' At the time I felt like what she was saying was so unfair to her dad. I thought, *Grow up! This is his life.* When I experienced those same feelings when my mom remarried after my dad died, then I understood. I realized this must be a common feeling. So I would say be patient, and realize that those feelings are going to be there. Give new stepfamily members a chance to prove themselves one way or another. Don't let your own emotions mar the relationship you could have. If I had stayed bitter, it would have been sad for my mom. If I had continued acting the way I did at the beginning of her remarriage, I would have missed out on a lot of happiness. Be patient; let them love each other." Bitterness hurts the embittered more than anyone else and may lead to false judgments.

Being critical of your mom or dad and your stepparent when they react inappropriately (in your opinion) to a situation judges them without understanding. Then you have a similar experience and have an "Aha!" moment. A light turns on and you see clearly what you did not see previously. Now you can sympathize with them, or you receive comfort knowing that others have had similar feelings or reactions. Your new perspective enriches your level of understanding. Withhold judgment of stepparents and allow personalities time to manifest themselves. Watch the evidence mount, building a case of sincere love and loyalty.

Faulty Impressions

Sandy also worked through her feelings toward her mother. Sandy described her feelings after her mother married: "I was mom's whole world. Mom made each of us children feel like that throughout our lives. We were everything to her. After her remarriage, I felt like my mom didn't love me anymore—like something was lost. It was that childish. It took a couple of months to get over my childishness and again feel my mom's loving, caring nature."

Initial impressions lead to misjudgments. Because Sandy recognized her childish reaction, she changed her judgment. Evidence of her mother's love outweighed Sandy's preliminary feelings of being replaced. Witnessing her mother's happiness increased Sandy's happiness. "Joy flows over into any relationship. When you see someone who is so happy, it brings you happiness. I also gained a caring dad that I really never had," Sandy said.

Be patient and wait for the case to unfold. Each piece of evidence increases understanding. Each judgment withheld in your stepfamily relationships allows you to be fair in your conclusions. Several years passed before Shirley's stepdaughters overcame their initial impression and changed their verdict. The girls didn't have much of a relationship with their dad before he married Shirley. Shirley encouraged Nolan to call his daughters, to visit them by himself, and to help them with projects. Slowly, the girls noticed and appreciated Shirley's efforts to encourage a relationship with their dad. The girls also noticed Shirley's sincerity in her relationship with their dad. They now judge Shirley more fairly.

Unknown Past

Unknown experiences may also cause erroneous judgments that adversely affect your relationships. Katie and her sisters make allowance for their stepmother's childhood experience without judging her. Katie said that something in her stepmother's past causes her to be skeptical of others, always judging their motives: "I don't think Beverly had unconditional love growing up because she needs it so much now." Katie accepts Beverly for who she is and tries to be fair by not judging. Katie and her sisters have learned how to maintain a relationship with their father without offending their stepmother. Their total acceptance and withholding judgment of their stepmother helped Beverly to overcome some preconceived notions and to judge Katie and her sisters fairly.

Inaccurate judgments obscure your view of reality just like storm clouds obscure the view of the sun. The sun eventually peeks out just as reality eventually sinks in, unveiling misjudgments. Guard against childish or other undesirable feelings that creep in and cloud your judgment. Withhold judgment and wait for time to reveal your stepparent's true personality.

Praise Versus Criticism

"I have yet to find the man, however exalted his station, who did not do better work and put forth greater effort under a spirit of approval than under a spirit of criticism."
—*Charles M. Schwab*

Offering sincere praise is yet one more way to show your loyalty to Mom or Dad and your stepparent. Perhaps you recall a time in your life when you were praised for an outstanding musical performance, a game-winning play, or a perfect score on a test. Or perhaps you feel your life is mediocre having received no praise. Worse yet, you may be the victim of perpetual criticism. Contrast possible side effects of these three scenarios. In the first scenario, the individual develops high self-esteem and continues to excel in life. The individual in the second scenario plods along in life making do. The individual in the third scenario develops low self-esteem and may wonder why try when she fails at everything. Each of these affects relationships by encouraging or diminishing feelings of loyalty.

Trudie recalled her stepmother expressing disapproval of some of her siblings: "I felt that Helen's negative comments were inappropriate. She entered our family as a stranger, then criticized my brothers' behavior. Even if their behavior was rude, it was not Helen's place to criticize them, especially to me. I refrained from visiting my dad and Helen so I wouldn't be accused of the same behavior." Critical remarks invariably weaken friendships with stepparents, making them vulnerable to natural consequences. Often the harm is unseen until the disaster occurs. Criticism of Trudie's brothers squelched any desire she had of visiting her dad and stepmother. She said a couple of years passed before visiting her dad's home.

Learning to control your tongue can be a lifelong pursuit. Like Thumper said in the movie *Bambi*, "If you can't say somethin' nice, don't say nothin' at all." Words of praise strengthen friendships, whereas criticism often weakens them. Praise offers stability and protects against natural disasters that buffet relationships. Look for ways to offer sincere praise to your stepparent in your efforts to forge a friendship.

Katie looks for the positive in her dad's wife: "I just try to let Beverly be herself. She is good at arts and crafts projects, so I'll ask her about her projects. Most of us in the family try to find positive things about Beverly and not say the negative. On the other hand, Beverly has a more negative personality and talks about a sibling behind their back."

Katie's brother struggles with being cordial to his step-mother. "Jason tends to be critical, and Beverly is also," Katie explained. "They criticize each other. My sisters and I try not to rock the boat too much, but Jason doesn't mind rocking the boat. Now the two try to stay clear of each other." Criticism severely strained their relationship.

Sustained criticism limits the desire for a friendship, and it blinds you to the abilities of those criticized. It may lead to suspicion and mistrust. Criticism gives a feeling of rejection rather than acceptance, whereas acknowledging feelings and abilities of stepparents and praising them opens your eyes to their talents. Praise is kind and expresses acceptance. Sustained praise leads to cherished friendships.

Criticism has a ripple effect much like a stone dropped in water. Criticism spoken to one family member may be repeated to another and another. Criticism often deteriorates the relationship between two people and may spread to other family members. Praise also has a ripple effect with a happier outcome. Praise may also be shared with one family member then another. Praise builds self-esteem, develops loyalty, and fortifies relationships.

Figuring Out the New Extended Family

Blending families is one decision of your parent and stepparent where you can wield great influence. If you don't want to blend, you don't have to blend. You just don't show up for combined family functions. It's as easy as that. But is isolation what you really want?

Blending families is difficult enough when children are young, but it presents unique challenges when they are adults. In today's society, families are more spread out than in previous generations. Proximity makes it difficult to get together often. Large families struggle to arrange everyone's schedules to be together at the same time or in a place that accommodates everyone. Differing personalities and family needs pose challenges. Some parents have tried to blend their families and have found that there are too many obstacles to make it worthwhile. If your mom or dad and stepparent want to blend their families, make an effort to support them by attending family activities. You maintain peace in your relationships, and you may end up with new friends.

Katie's father and stepmother tried to integrate their families, but distance proved a hindrance. "Dad and Beverly tried a little bit at first to blend their families, but trying to get that many people together is difficult. It's tough enough trying to get our family together," Katie said. "Family members live across the state, so coordinating schedules with travel time is tricky."

Life is so busy that siblings sometimes find it challenging to keep in touch with each other, let alone spend time together. Some adult children cooperate with their parents to attend combined family activities but have little desire to develop relationships with stepsiblings beyond the perfunctory appearances. Life is too stressful and hectic to try to add just one more person to your contact list. Besides it's not like these other people are really your family. Or are they?

At the beginning of their marriage, Diane's mother and Jim tried to blend their families, but it was short-lived. Diane described her feelings: "Jim is my mom's husband; that's his relation to me. I don't think any of my brothers or sisters spent a lot of time with him. My mom especially tried to make an effort to blend the families. Mom introduced us to Jim's children by saying, 'This is your new stepbrother or this is your stepsister.' We were all in our twenties, thirties, and forties. We don't consider Jim's children our stepbrothers and stepsisters. They are Jim's kids and we're her kids, and we don't do things with them. They are nice people but it is not like we are going to live together under the same roof and have a sibling relationship. Since then my mom has made an effort to keep Jim's relationship with his children going because he is not very good at that."

The terms "stepmother," "stepfather," and "stepsibling" connote some type of familial affinity. The word "stepfamily" conjures pictures of a mom and dad with dependent children still living in the same house, at least part of the time. As Diane said, adult stepchildren rarely live under the same roof, so referring to each other as stepbrother or stepsister feels awkward. Feeling comfortable interacting is challenging for stepsiblings who were not raised together and who feel like strangers. Being spread out across the country and having few opportunities to interact make it difficult to establish anything more than a casual acquaintance. Quite often the only bond between adult children of a mature remarried couple is that they happen to share the same (step)parents.

Successful Blending

In spite of all the odds against them, some mature stepfamilies succeed in blending their families. Kristen said that her dad and Mary successfully blended their combined thirteen children. Mary took over the writing of Nick's weekly family newsletter, which she sends to each child in both families. The newsletter helps everyone get acquainted and stay in touch. Mary makes a calendar every year that includes birthdays, anniversaries, and special events of all the extended family and uses pictures of a different child's family each month. The children call each other or send cards for special occasions. They have an annual family reunion that everyone attends. Nick's and Mary's children feel like they are getting to know each other and are comfortable together.

Life in general often takes bizarre twists and turns. The same holds true with sibling and stepsibling relationships.

After the divorce of Abby's parents and subsequent death of her father, Abby and her brother and sister had little interaction. Yet Abby describes her relationship with a stepbrother and his wife as "friendly." She said, "They asked if we would be the guardians of their children if something should happen to them. My stepsister is the one I have seen and interacted with the most. We have a closeness that comes and goes depending on her behaviors and how I react to them."

Effort and desire are the primary ingredients in successfully blending families. Sometimes stepsiblings hit it off and become good friends, making blending easy and rewarding. Other times people work at developing endearing ties, making blending a chore that may offer advantages if enough effort is put forth. There are even those who have no desire to interact with stepsiblings and would not recognize them if they passed on the street. The choice is yours. If you don't want to blend, you cannot be forced. That is okay. You know your lifestyle and time commitments better than anyone else, so you are best able to judge what you are willing and able to commit to relationships. Your desires may change as your circumstances change. When the desire is there, then you'll make an effort.

Intimacy Versus Isolation

The intimacy versus isolation stage of Erikson's psychosocial-emotional development describes a young adult's experience with true intimacy, whether it be a good marriage or a genuine friendship. Those unable to achieve either one usually experience isolation. Many parent/child relationships evolve to friendship as the children mature to adulthood. A remarriage weakens parent/child bonds when children feel those ties threatened by divided loyalties. Feeling betrayed, children withdraw from family social interaction, resulting in isolation. On the other hand, vigilance to family loyalties maintains or achieves intimacy. Loyalty to your parents assures them of your constant love. You maintain familial intimacy. Loyalty to their moral teachings manifested through upright behavior toward your stepparent honors your parents and stepparent. You develop a genuine friendship. Loyalty to personal values allows you to feel comfortable with achieving personal intimacy. You can help increase intimacy by increasing expressions of praise and appreciation, by planning activities to do together, and by sharing dreams and aspirations. This should be done in small amounts over time. Too much at one time will make people feel smothered.

Take Action

If you find yourself in a situation similar to Jack's children, you may feel abandoned when your parent sides with his or her spouse, forming a conspiracy against you. Here are specific steps you can take to reconcile relationships:

> Consider your attitude and behavior, examining them for any indication of disrespect. If you find you need improvement, change your attitude and adjust your behavior to fit your desires. Replace character flaws preventing you from respecting stepparents with respectful traits to begin developing friendships. Recognize that a normal developmental process for a stepfamily is for parents to protect and nurture their marriage. Extend a peace offering by apologizing, then be kind and considerate. If your parent or stepparent is totally at fault, then be patient as you model the respect you desire.

> Consider your parent and stepparent. Put yourself in their shoes. Withhold judgment as you try to understand their actions. Remember they are adjusting to new situations and roles as well. People may behave irrationally or unpredict-

ably due to stress and insecurity. You may want to give them some space and time for adjustment.

In case of an ultimatum given to your parent by your stepparent, "me or your children," it might be best to back away for a while. Keep in touch with Mom or Dad with e-mails or with a friendly phone call now and then.

Possible Scenario
Because of your parent's behavior and choices, you no longer feel you are a priority to Mom or Dad. You long to know where loyalties lie. Adapt the following scenario to your relationship with your parent.

Child: Mom (or Dad), I was heartbroken when you refused to take care of my daughter while I took Jimmy to the emergency room.

Parent: I'm sorry, honey. We had plans to go to dinner.

Child: But you've always been available when I needed you in the past. Now I feel like our family is at the bottom of your priorities. Who can I count on for help?

Parent: I want you to feel you can count on me. That night we were celebrating our first anniversary, and I was torn between the two. I thought about you all evening. How can I make it up to you?

The Heart of the Matter
Central longings for intimacy in family life are partially fulfilled through loyalty. Loyalty has the power to make or break family ties. Remarried parents walk a fine line trying to balance loyalty to a new spouse and loyalty to two sets of children.

Adults discover no discrepancy between honoring a stepparent and remaining loyal to their parents when they adhere to moral teachings and behavior taught and modeled throughout their lives.

- Show your loyalty to your parents by honoring their moral teachings. Offer a sense of safety and security by being available to help them when challenges arise. Appreciate loyalty in your parent.
- Courtesy, or lack thereof, affects your relationships.Little acts of kindness foster friendships by making life pleasant and encourage you to spend time together. Common courtesies inspire a personal regard for each other and guards against the buffetings of misunderstanding, mistrust, and hostility. Be polite with your words and actions. Overlook rude behavior, and don't speak of it to others. Be pleasant to be around. If you need to unload hurt feelings, do it with a trusted friend or counselor. Take a lot of deep breaths and expect the best from others—you usually get what you expect. Strive to develop a friendship with your stepparent through courteous behavior.
- Replace negative feelings with thoughts of loyalty, and treat stepparents with respect. Esteem your stepparent for his or her position as your parent's spouse. Respect your stepparent's feelings and honor invisible boundaries. Replace suspicion by listening attentively and expressing your opinions tactfully. If you experience a decaying relationship with your mom or dad and your stepparent, begin taking preventative measures.
- Accept the kindness extended by your parent and stepparent to invite you to participate in family functions. Take the initiative to reciprocate invitations. Or better yet, be the first to include them in social activities—sooner rather than later. The longer you hold onto feelings of

exclusion and alienation, the harder it is to reach out and to include those who caused the pain. Invite your parent and stepparent to pertinent happenings in your family to nurture your friendship.

- Withhold judgment of a stepparent until you gather evidence. Be fair and let the evidence speak for itself. Gather information through observation and a willingness to listen for understanding. Settle disputes quickly without judging. Let go of initial impressions when they are inaccurate. Evidence may indicate a loving and supportive stepparent. Make allowance for unknown experiences in your stepparent's past that may affect behavior. Seek the help of a trusted, unbiased mutual friend, relative, or a professional if emotions are too high. You can find a list of professional marriage and family therapists in your area at the American Association for Marriage and Family Therapy's Web site (*www.aamft.org*).

- Refrain from criticizing your stepparent. Recognize and acknowledge his or her contributions to your family. Look for your stepparent's talents and abilities and express sincere compliments. Let words of praise permeate conversations with your stepparent, cheering them and promoting loving friendships.

- If your parent and stepparent want to blend their families, support them by joining activities or planning one yourself, such as writing a family newsletter or scheduling a holiday celebration. If desirable, include a stepparent's children in your family activities. Try to get to know them as you have occasion to interact. Do whatever your family enjoys doing together and invite your stepparent's family to join in if you desire a relationship with them.

CHAPTER 7

"Why Didn't You Ask Before You Sold My Mom's China?"

"Your living is determined not so much by what life brings you as by the attitude you bring to life; not so much by what happens to you as by the way your mind looks at what happens."
—*Lewis L. Dunnington*

Family inheritance issues, whether a large estate with financial holdings or the family home and a few heirlooms, are never easy. Inheritance squabbles have torn families apart. Children refuse to speak to Mom or Dad, or siblings have nothing to do with one another because Johnny wound up with Dad's coin collection or Susie received Mom's china. Drama unfolds before your eyes, and you thought your family was immune to such trivialities. Add a new spouse to the mix, and the drama crescendos.

Life seemed simple while Mom and Dad were either alive or together as a couple. They worked hard to accomplish their dream of owning a home and providing for their needs and desires in retirement years. Perhaps they prepared legal documents to ensure proper handling of their finances after their death. Then the inevitable happened—one of your parents died or they divorced and their hopes and dreams vanished—replaced with different dreams with a new spouse.

Since the wedding, many of the newlyweds' decisions probably affected your life, such as their place of residence. Their financial decisions and retirement activities may be contrary to your parent's original decisions. You wonder if Mom or Dad will spend your inheritance on a new house or squander it on a new spouse. Will expenses be covered fairly and equitably, or should they be? What if one spouse has more money than the other one? Will you still be remembered in the will or be cut out completely? Will you still receive the antique vanity you were promised? It would be nice to have some say in their decisions, but ultimately, the decisions belong to your parent and stepparent since it is their residence, their finances, and their personal belongings.

But don't sit back and do nothing. If they haven't already spoken with a lawyer, encourage your parent and stepparent to meet with an attorney to put their financial and legal matters in order according to their desires. Legal documents to protect themselves and their interests include prenuptial agreements, wills, powers of attorney, and health care directives. An asset protection attorney can explain the ramifications of marriage to the couple and the importance of each document to protect their individual needs and assets. In an article published in the *Elder Law Journal*, Joanna Lyn Grama penned, "a well-thought-out marriage supported by legal documentation can allow elders the happiness of a worry-free marriage."

The conflict arises with our sense of what is right and fair. An important question to ask is: What is most important to you, your relationship with your parent or material possessions? Other questions arise that may not have a definitive answer. For example, if the two enter the marriage with approximately equal estates, is it fair to combine their assets and divide them equally among their children? Possibly. Is it right for a stepfather to sell your dad's personal belongings or for a stepmother to give your mother's collectibles to her children? Probably not. What do you do when your stepparent puts his or her name on the title of your parent's home, then bequeaths it to his or her children? That appears wrong, unjust, and unfair. You may consider hiring a lawyer to protect Mom or Dad's and your interests. These issues are definitely sticky and tricky, yet some families resolve them amicably.

Regardless of your parent's decisions, you still have options available to you. How do you handle their financial decisions when you disagree with them? You are best equipped to answer that question since you are acquainted with the situation and ramifications. Be aware that remodeling homes and altering wills are common practices, especially as relationships evolve. Be sensitive to your emotional reactions, examine the fundamental trigger, and consider the intent behind decisions. Remember, your relationship is with your parent and not financial holdings.

Dad's House, Her House, or Somewhere Else?

A primary concern of newlyweds is where to live. Often, mature remarried couples own separate houses, which affords them several choices for a place of residence. They could sell or rent one house and live in the other, sell both and buy a new one, or keep both and jump back and forth. Couples consider their preferences, proximity to family, and ease in caring for themselves as they age, among other issues. Your desires may or may not figure in their decision. You know they can make their own decisions, but you have an active interest since their choices affect you and possibly your inheritance. Real estate is usually the most valuable asset a person owns; therefore, what your parent and stepparent do with their house(s) could have long-term effects. An awareness of some of the effects of their decisions is beneficial. Here are a few examples of decisions couples made.

Mike's dad, Frank, was still living in the home where Mike grew up when he married Nadine and she moved into his house. "Nadine had lived in my dad's neighborhood before her divorce," Mike said. Nadine moved back among her friends, a bonus for her. They avoided rent and mortgage, which fit Frank's frugal nature. They were in close proximity to their children living in the area.

A **Parent's** Perspective

Marie and John both had a home. They decided to sell his and live in hers. "Then we discovered we wanted to live in the country. We bought a lovely home, with a lot of acreage, that we enjoy." Marie welcomed her children and stepchildren into their home to help them feel comfortable when visiting, "I let our children know they are always welcome in our home, that it is their dad's home as well as mine. Some of our children come and stay for three weeks in the summer. I treat them all like family, because we are a family."

Sandy's stepdad, Dean, sold his home to move in with Sandy's mom, Elaine, after they married. He sacrificed attendance at grandchildren's sports events and proximity to some of his children to make his wife happy. Elaine remained close to her children and friends, where she was comfortable. Sandy was impressed with Dean's concern for her mom.

Valerie's mom and stepdad sold both their residences to purchase a house across town. They found that it didn't feel like home because they were further away from their families. They eventually sold that house, opting to live closer to family.

Making Sense of Your Reactions

Perhaps you can relate to two of Neal's children who visited less often after their dad moved into his new wife's home. It isn't comfortable visiting Mom or Dad in someone else's house or seeing a different man or woman in your parents' home. You wonder whether you should knock or just walk in, especially if they are living in your childhood home. Mom's presence and influence in the house is noticeably absent. Or Dad's belongings disappeared. Should you ask to use the restroom facilities or for a drink or are you free to make yourself at home as you've always done? That depends on your relationship with Mom or Dad and your stepparent. It may change with time. Play it by ear. Visiting may feel so uncomfortable that you limit your time or frequency. That could be heartbreaking to parents.

Your reaction to your parent's housing decision can vary from being uncomfortable to feeling totally at ease, and it depends a lot on the frequency of your visits. Moms have a way of making anywhere feel like home, a place where you are always welcome. Mom's influence, personality, and personal touches follow her from home to home. Mom generally makes her residence feel warm and inviting. Initially, visiting may be awkward when a man other than your dad is there. Visiting Dad, even if it's your childhood home, is a different matter. Not only is another woman sharing your dad's residence, but everything has changed. Dad's new wife added her personal effects while removing your mother's personal touches. It definitely doesn't feel like home—but more like visiting an extended relative.

Steve's mom lived in the same house for thirty years. While widowed, she built a new house that Nolan moved into after they married. Steve explained, "Even though I have no memories in Mom's new house, it still feels comfortable and like home. I don't have anxieties or tension visiting."

Melanie and her son lived with her mom, Alice, while she was dating Dan. Alice moved into Dan's apartment, then they bought a home to accommodate Dan's aging parents. When Dan retired, they moved into Alice's home, which was Melanie's childhood home. "It was an interesting phenomenon for me visiting them. After I married, I thought it would be really weird—not going to my home, my hometown, my mom's house. Later we visited them in the little town where I grew up. But I discovered that it didn't matter what house Mom lived in, because home is where my mother is. I felt comfortable. I never felt like I was intruding in Dan's space."

Melanie's friendship with Dan began during the courtship. Melanie's first visit after her mom and Dan's wedding caught her off guard since she was no longer the center of her mom's attention. Melanie accepted the change as a natural evolution of her mom's marital status. Dan's welcoming nature and her mom's presence made each residence feel like home. Melanie said her brother had an opposite reaction. It's interesting that siblings raised in the same environment can be so different.

What about visiting Dad? Megan described her reaction to a visit to her dad and his wife: "Our family home changed into 'their' home. We had always gone in and out as kids would normally do even after we left home. After Dad married, we felt like we should knock rather than use our key. Dad met my brother and me at the door one time and told us it wasn't a good time to visit. It felt like a slap in the face. My brother and I were stunned. It seemed that we were locked out." Of course, Megan was hurt by her dad's refusal to receive her and her brother. Who wouldn't be? Understanding was not immediately forthcoming for Megan, but it eventually came.

Sometimes comprehension comes when we least expect it and from sources unrelated to the situation. Several years passed before Megan understood her father's unwelcome greeting. "At the time it was a surprise. It would have been nice to have it explained, but I eventually got the picture. Years later a neighbor lady explained to me that she had the locks changed on her doors because she wanted to have the freedom to wear or not to wear what she wanted in her house without having her grown children surprise her by just showing up and walking in. 'Aha!' I said to myself. That's what my dad and his wife wanted—their own place! It was a new border being drawn on a home that was no longer ours. With grown, moved-out kids, parents, especially new ones, would like to enjoy the home with the security of knowing it is private and protected."

Differences between visiting Mom and Dad can be partially explained by the traditional roles of men and women. Family scholars generally assert that women are socialized into maintaining relationships, whereas men are socialized first into working. Therefore, moms tend to be considerate of your comfort when you visit and attentive to your needs, while dads may be clueless to why you might feel ill at ease visiting. Things will never be the same as they were when Mom and Dad were together; however, as you spend more time in your parent's home and with your stepparent, your comfort level increases.

Who Gets the House?

Underlying the emotional adjustment of a stranger in your home or visiting your parent in a strange house is the question, "Who gets the house when one or both die?" Herein lies the importance of the prenuptial agreement, if there was one. Some children presume they will be the natural heirs of their parents' estate, especially if they are so designated in their wills. That was *before* Mom or Dad remarried and invested the proceeds from the sale of the family home out of your reach. How unfair! It's rightfully yours! Or is it?

Your parents worked hard to buy their home. When it is sold, the money is theirs to do with as they choose. But to invest it in someone else's house or to squander it on another spouse, how dare they! Take a deep breath and consider the matter. Your parents have the right to spend their money how they choose. They don't need your permission. Their needs are still a primary concern.

For example, Nolan used personal funds to finish the basement of Shirley's house to make it more comfortable for them. Since the house remains in Shirley's name to be inherited by her children, Nolan's daughters, as his heirs, receive no benefit. Steve admitted Nolan's daughters could resent that decision.

Some people become attached to a particular house and prefer things to remain as they have always been, partly because they find it difficult to adjust to change. One daughter told her mother, "If you remodel your house, I won't come and visit." Her aunt replied, "Are you visiting your mom or the house?" That was an appropriate reminder that children's priority should be their relationship with their parent rather than a house or other material possession. All homes need remodeling or redecorating at one point or another. but sometimes the timing of the changes is inconsiderate of your feelings.

Most men leave the decorating to their wives. An interior designer in my community indicated that 85 to 90 percent of the requests for her services come from women. Women desire to make their home their castle, a place where they are comfortable. In remarriages, many women remove items of the previous wife and redecorate with their own personal touches. However, you may feel the sting of too many changes too quickly. This was the case with Mike. In a six-month period, new carpeting, flooring, and window hangings were installed in his dad's house, and new furniture purchased. Hardly any reminder of Mike's mother remained. With physical reminders of his mother gone, so was the feeling of being home. Still, Mike continued to visit his dad and stepmother, and he is more comfortable now.

Richard's stepmother, Nancy, moved into his dad's home. They remodeled the kitchen and made other changes. Richard said it still felt like home to him, but his wife, Dana, felt a different ambience to the home with the influence of Richard's mother gone. Dana finally felt comfortable visiting her mother-in-law, then she had to adjust to a new woman and all the renovations. Richard said, "I didn't necessarily have a problem with the changes. I still felt the same visiting."

A **Stepparent's** Perspective
Patricia said that she planned to follow the example of her Uncle Calvin's wife, Audrey. When they married, Audrey moved into Calvin's home. She left it virtually untouched in its interior decorating. She wanted the influence of Calvin's first wife to remain in the house, including pictures of her so that Calvin's children would still feel like it was home and want to visit often. Audrey added her own taste to the home décor when they moved to another state. Even then Audrey retained some influence of the first wife.

Anxious to make their new abode their home, some women make changes with little regard to their impact on you. Such was true with Trudie. She overheard her new stepmother tell another relative, "I've made some changes in the home. The children don't like it, but I had to make it mine." Trudie added, "It's not that I don't like the changes. They are nice, but Helen took my mother's influence completely out of the home. I don't like the feeling of being in a stranger's house. In making it her home, I have no part of it."

Misperceptions are common and may go unaddressed if you are uncomfortable discussing them with your stepparent. Addressing the misperceptions calmly and lovingly facilitates understanding, often resolves the misperceptions, and provides a means of becoming better acquainted. Effort to resolve misperceptions demonstrates a desire to improve your relationship. In the process, your stepparent may become your friend. Changes occur even when a man moves into his wife's house. The wife wants her husband to feel comfortable, so pictures or possessions of her first husband, your dad, may disappear. The new husband may not notice the changes, but as the child you are keenly aware of them.

Sandy's mother decorates with family photos: "They're everywhere—upstairs, downstairs, in the hallway. That's about the only thing that's on my mom's wall. Wherever she can put a picture, she's got one!" Initially, Sandy was offended when a picture of her father disappeared: "We had a big family picture taken that hangs on my mother's wall. My dad was sick at the time the picture was taken and wasn't in it, so my mom cut out a little photo of him and put it to the side of her head on the picture. After Mom remarried, she removed dad's picture. That was probably the hardest change for me. I wondered what that meant about me. Do I not exist? He wasn't a model of a wonderful husband or father, but he was still my dad. All of a sudden he was gone out of our home, out of our lives. It seemed like Mom wanted to erase him. Those were my first childish feelings. After thinking about it for a while, I realized it was important for Mom to remove Dad's picture because it might be uncomfortable for her husband having pictures of my dad in the house."

Sandy handled the situation wisely. She considered why her mother removed the picture and her stepfather's feelings. Sandy mentally worked through her feelings and began to understand that her mother had Dean's interest at heart and wanted him to be comfortable in her home, now his as well—another verification of a woman's concern for the emotional comfort of family, in this case her husband. Dean might be ill at ease with his predecessor's photos and belongings throughout the house. Once Sandy understood that, she was okay with the changes. Thinking through it rationally helped Sandy to accept that she was still part of the family and her mother still loved her.

Little by little Mom's possessions and influence are removed or Dad's things disappear. Similar situations may cause you to wonder about your identity in your parent's new marital situation. Changes, whether subtle or obvious, affect you. Obviously, it is the couple's decision as to what redecorating occurs. But once the decision is made they have no control over your feelings or reactions. My interviews revealed that many children are offended and uncomfortable. Some mentally process their reactions to put them in the proper perspective; they try to understand their parent's behavior and decision. This unselfish behavior indicates maturity, wisdom, and a desire to pursue good relationships.

Change is inevitable after a remarriage regardless of where the couple lives. Knowing that and experiencing the changes are two different things. Visiting may be uncomfortable at the beginning, but continue to visit and offer love and support. In time you adjust and become more comfortable visiting Mom or Dad in the new or redecorated residence.

Material Possessions

The returning or disappearance of photos is one example of behavior that emotes negative reactions. A different experience may cause feelings of betrayal or rejection for you. Dad's guitar may be given to a step-grandson desiring to play the guitar. Mom's collector spoons, some of which you gave to her, might be sold at a garage sale in an effort to clean up. Your third-grade ceramic handprint might be tossed in the garbage. The monetary value of some items is insignificant, while others are quite valuable, such as paintings or antiques. Yet, regardless, the

133

sentimental value is incalculable. Is it too much to ask that you be consulted before any willy-nilly dispensing of Mom or Dad's personal possessions, some of which were gifts from you?

Whether the issue be returning photos, selling dad's golf clubs, or wearing clothing you gave to your mother, the principle of handling it is the same—what is most important to you, the relationship or the item? Another question to ponder is what angers you most, the loss of potential possession of the item or your stepparent's seeming disregard of your interest and desire? Offenses occur, usually unintentionally. Reflexive actions are rarely beneficial; more often they are counterproductive to happy relationships. Keep your stepparent's behavior and decisions (as well as your own) in proper perspective, make the relationship the priority, and act in ways that promote harmony.

When your parent remarries, there is no guarantee where or with whom the family treasures will end up. Roger told me that his cousins expected to receive family heirlooms. Then their mother died and their father remarried. The new stepmother began giving valuable family treasures to her children as gifts, crushing the expectations of Roger's cousins. However, the stepmother's children were thrilled with the valuable heirlooms. If the heirlooms are significant to them, Roger's cousins could discuss it with their dad, their stepmother, or even her children with the hope of an amicable resolution.

Taylor arrived at his dad's home one day to find his stepmother wearing a dress Taylor gave to his mother. He may have felt like screaming out, "What are you doing? How can you be so insensitive? Do you realize I gave that dress to my mother?" But instead Taylor tried to ignore it. His stepmother could have been elated to be the same size as her predecessor and to inherit a new wardrobe, not thinking of the memories or feelings wearing the clothing would invoke in her stepchildren.

Trudie asked her dad for childhood games and souvenirs that she had left at his home. Her dad and stepmother donated them to a secondhand store. Trudie could have overreacted, bawling out, "Those are my things! You have no right to donate them! What were you thinking?" But she dismissed it as trivial in comparison to the relationship. Since her parents stored the items for more than twenty years without Trudie mentioning them, her dad supposed she was not interested in them.

Material possessions are insignificant in comparison to family relationships. Possessions can be replaced; it may be expensive, but it is possible. On the other hand, people cannot be replaced. After the death of a loved one, the truth of that reality is poignant. Focus on living family members, making your relationships a priority. Mom or Dad, whether divorced or widowed, will not be around forever. Control your emotions by focusing on loving behaviors.

Personal Finances

You may wonder why Dad has money for expensive vacations when he didn't with your mother or why Mom is extravagant in redecorating her home when it wasn't a concern to her previously. Do they realize they are spending your inheritance? They probably do. They also recognize something you may have forgotten—it is their money to do with as they wish and so desire. Mature couples' financial needs are different from those of young newlyweds or couples raising children. Rather than budgeting to pay a mortgage, they may budget to afford prescriptions. Many remarried couples have greater disposable income than they had while raising their family. Financial decisions are more diverse than housing options, but each carries a price tag. Once again, you may be excluded from participating in their decision.

Melanie said, "When my mom and Dan married, she kept her money in a separate account, but Dan's assets became joint property. His money is her money. That might be common in a lot of older couple marriages—for women what's mine is mine, and what's yours is ours." This stems from the traditional role of men being cast as provider. Many continue in that role when they remarry. They are happy to have a wife who loves them and cares for them. Many men willingly take care of the financial needs, allowing their wives to keep whatever savings or investments they have. If this is your mother, you are probably grateful that she has someone to take care of her. If this is your dad, you may be raising your eyebrows, wondering "What next?"

Some parents inform their children of financial decisions and others keep them private. Steve is well informed of his mother's finances: "My mom and Nolan are both financially comfortable and have their own nest egg or retirement fund. A couple of things are probably worth pointing out. They have kept separate accounts, including checking accounts. But then they have a joint account. Each contributes an agreed-upon amount of money to deposit into this joint account to pay for household expenses. But what's funny is when my mom takes us on a trip, it comes out of her funds—not their funds. If Nolan wants to buy a gift for us for Christmas, that comes out of his funds. They use their own money for discretionary items. Nolan has taken us all out for dinner at times with his funds. Nobody feels like somebody is stealing from somebody else. The whole idea of inheritance is sticky in some situations. When men spend a lot of money on a new woman, some children have a hard time with that if their dad didn't do it for their mother. I've seen it in numerous situations."

Apparently, Steve's mom and stepdad have tried to reduce potential friction with their children. Their concern for fairness is evident by maintaining separate accounts for personal expenses. When the inevitable occurs, their separate accounts will be in tact, minimizing potential problems among their children. They carry their fairness a step further by contributing an equal amount to a joint account for monthly expenses. They live in the same house and eat the same food, so it is reasonable that they would share utility and food expenses. This system is also an equitable way for couples to handle finances when both have sufficient funds to care for themselves.

Some parents and stepparents make promises that fairness will be their standard. After saying, "I do," that promise becomes null and void. Before marrying Katie's dad and moving into his home, Beverly told her husband-to-be, "Oh, what's yours is yours and what's mine is mine. We'll keep it all separate." After the wedding, Beverly sold her home and made sure her name was on the papers for her husband's house. Katie has taken everything in stride and acknowledges that Beverly spends a lot more money than her dad, but she's also done things to fix up their house. "We're not expecting anything when dad dies. He owns the house but it's not like we can get Beverly out of it. So let them figure out their finances," Katie said.

Parents may reprimand their children for saying one thing then doing the opposite, and then they do the same thing. They say and do dumb things without thinking, just like anyone else in love. You think they would know better with their many years of experience. Rather than being bothered by the broken promise or with inheritance issues, Katie focused on her relationship with her dad and Beverly. Accept prenuptial promises of parents with a grain of salt (unless they are included in a legally binding document such as a prenuptial agreement) knowing that feelings and opinions change over time and as relationships develop. Be amenable to financially helping out your mom or dad and your stepparent occasionally, as Katie has, if the need arises. If you are in a financial position to do so, what a blessing it is to help them after their sacrifices for you throughout your life.

Some children are clueless of their parent's financial affairs. Money is one of two topics that is taboo to discuss, yet it is the cause of many familial disagreements. Mike's dad keeps his financial affairs private. Mike said, "Concerning my dad's finances, I don't have any idea. My dad has always kept finances to himself. He always handled the finances in our family. I never knew how much money we had or didn't have, and I still don't. I don't have a clue if they have any prenuptial agreements or wills. So if I don't get anything from my dad, then I don't get anything from my dad."

You don't need to know the details of your parents' financial situation, but it is nice when they inform you of their intentions as well as changes made to wills throughout the marriage. Doing so reduces the risk of unexpected surprises when death occurs.

Wills

Regardless of age, marital relationships evolve over time. What seemed just and fair before marriage or during the first year may no longer be valid after three, five, or ten years of marriage. The couple's love, care, and concern for each other deepens the longer they are married. It is only natural to want to provide for the other's welfare in the event of death. Most couples try to make prudent financial decisions according to their present and future needs. As needs change and the relationship matures, decisions change. Wills are updated to accommodate revised desires. You may still be included in the will or be left out completely. You could even be pleasantly surprised by the turn of events.

Melanie's stepfather, Dan, had his will rewritten to include Melanie and her brother as well as retaining his two children in it. "I didn't think he had to include us. It might stem from him feeling closer to my mom's kids than he does to his own children." Melanie did not set out to be included in Dan's will. She focused on her relationship with her mom and Dan. The frequent contact through phone calls, e-mails, and visits indicated Melanie's love for her mom and Dan. Including Melanie in his will is one way for Dan to reciprocate the love he felt.

As an only child, Richard was named executor of his dad's estate. Richard said that before the wedding, his father, George, made a big deal about how he and Nancy were going to maintain their separate finances with estates. Richard wanted to believe his dad but he allowed for the evolution of his dad's marital relationship and possible will changes: "Dad modified that position several times over the years. Every time he makes a change, he tells me about it. Now it's to the point where Dad and Nancy have integrated everything they own as joint property. When Dad passes on, there will be some gifts to my children, but the bulk of his estate will go to Nancy. My wife feels like Dad made some commitments when they announced their plans to get married and now they've changed. I know Dad was entirely sincere when he made his promise; he just didn't realize feelings and plans might change over an appreciable amount of time. So my expectations weren't disappointed as Dad modified his will and financial situation. If I were in the same situation, I would be careful about what type of commitments I made to my children and make allowances for this relationship to evolve and not set up expectations about how things will be."

Knowing the natural progression of marriage and the desire to care for one's spouse doesn't necessarily make changes in your parent's will easier to accept. Will revisions could even create contention in your own marriage. You probably never dreamed that your parent's remarriage could become so complicated. Richard's dad kept him informed as alterations were made to his will. Some parents make changes without bothering to inform their children, who are caught unaware when the parent dies.

No two people react the same way. Just as Richard and his wife had opposing reactions, Sandy's mother made will changes that were an issue for one child but not for others. Sandy said, "My youngest sister is divorced and never had her own home. I think she expected to inherit Mom's house. The rest of us have our own home and we don't need another one. That sister is upset about Mom and Dean's wills and financial decisions. Originally, Mom's house was to be divided among us, and Dean's family wouldn't get anything. My mom didn't feel like that was fair since Dean used his money for their living expenses and to fix up their home, so they changed their wills to divide everything equally among all the kids. The rest of us think this is fair. Dean's children didn't think they would get anything. So I'm sure they felt good about it."

The old adage "You can please some of the people some of the time but you can't please all of the people all of the time" rings true. Someone is bound to be offended by will revisions, especially if they receive less than expected. The best parents can do is to try to be fair to everyone. No one can ask for anything more than that.

Sandy is content with the manner in which her mother and stepfather have handled their financial affairs and feels they've tried to be fair: "I feel like that is the only way to do it. Neither one had a lot. They are both living on social security. Mom and Dean came into the marriage with about the same, very little. They've done very well. They've had a lot of fun taking tours together. They've had a really good eight years, a happy eight years." Sandy doesn't expect anything; it's hard to divide up very little among twelve children. She is happy that her mother is enjoying life.

When parents desire to leave you an inheritance, establishing trusts and maintaining separate accounts reduces legal problems and taxes, especially in cases of an appreciable amount of wealth. Some couples sign prenuptial agreements to protect assets they desire to leave to their children, minimizing friction when death occurs, but wills are still essential. Some people marry with the intent to take advantage of financial assets. Perhaps that is your concern or your experience. What are your options, other than lengthy legal battles, if your parent married a "gold digger"? It depends on the laws of your state and whether your parent's legal documents are in order. Consult an attorney to learn your rights.

Financial decisions should be carefully considered based on your parent and stepparent's individual assets, their welfare, and their living expenses. Decisions will vary according to their needs and desires. Parents who know what they want for themselves, their spouse, and their children are wise to seek the professional counsel of an attorney to ensure that their wishes are carried out when death comes. Couples should consider setting up a trust and at the bare minimum having separate wills.

Industry Versus Inferiority

This phase of relationships seems to correlate with Erikson's industry versus inferiority. During their early school-age years children learn rules often through games or team sports in order to relate to their peers. They develop self-discipline to apply themselves to their studies and homework as they gain mastery of academic subjects. Rules apply to inheritance issues and affect how we relate to family members. Understanding the laws of your state may motivate you to encourage Mom or Dad to put her or his financial and legal affairs in order to be fair and just. Games go smoothly when everyone knows the rules and is willing to abide by them. Then no one feels cheated or inferior. While an unusual application of Erikson's stage of industry versus inferiority, this is an important issue. In my clinical practice I have witnessed many stepfamilies with adult children who were thrown into chaos because parents failed to take care of legal and inheritance issues.

Take Action

If your family situation is similar to Mike's in that you are clueless about the assets and financial decisions of your parent and stepparent, yet you are interested in knowing their intent and plans when they die, or if you are overly concerned about Mom or Dad's will, you could suggest holding a family meeting. As your parent's child, you would like to carry out Mom or Dad's wishes after death, so it would be helpful to know what they are. Offer to host it at your home or locate a neutral meeting room (city libraries often have rooms). During these meetings discuss desires, concerns, and potential problems. Airing these issues may help your parent and stepparent consider choices previously disregarded. They may choose to refine their legal documents to clarify their wishes. Long-term care may be one of the issues to consider, as it will become a priority in the not-to-distant future. A family meeting assures that everyone is informed, minimizing potential surprises. Consider employing the expertise of a financial planner to explain options to protect assets from unnecessary taxes, to preserve wealth for future generations, or to avoid prolonged legal action. Some of the benefits of a family meeting include being informed, reducing inheritance feuds, and having peace of mind that legal documents are in order.

An alternative approach is to meet with your parent privately or in conjunction with your stepparent to discuss their wills. Listen without offering advice unless solicited, and even then be cautious.

Recommend that your parent consult with an attorney to put his or her financial matters in order and offer to help. Or you could wait for your parent to approach you to discuss matters. If that doesn't happen, don't be disappointed.

Possible Scenario
You can broach financial or legal issues with your parent in numerous ways. Take into account your family dynamics and your comfort zone. Here is one possibility:

Child: Mom, I have been thinking about your new marriage and some of its legal ramifications. I want to help you ensure your desires are fulfilled if anything happens to you or your husband. Are your legal documents in order?

Parent: Well, your dad and I had wills written up before he died. But I may need to make some changes to mine.

Child: Have you considered returning to your attorney to make the changes? Now might be a good time to consider setting up separate trusts as well as establishing a long-term care fund or insurance.

Parent: That's a good idea, but my attorney is in a different city. Perhaps I could use my husband's attorney.

Child: One lawyer recommended that partners in a remarriage use different lawyers for their legal documents. If you would like me to help you find a lawyer and accompany you, I will arrange my schedule to do so.

Parent: I'll take you up on that offer. Legal issues can be tricky.

The Heart of the Matter

The decisions your mom or dad and your stepparent make, everything from their place of residence to changes in their wills, are likely to cause you to react emotionally. You may be surprised and be included in your stepparent's will or you could be devastated when cut from your parent's will. Keep your parent's decisions and your reactions in proper perspective. To maintain harmonious relationships, remember your relationship is with Mom or Dad, not possessions you hope to inherit. You may have little input into your parent's financial decisions, but you have great influence on your relationship with your mom or dad. Take action to shape the relationship you desire.

- Where your parent and stepparent live is their decision. Their needs and desires are the top priority. Undoubtedly, remodeling or redecorating occurs. Regardless of where they live or what changes they make, they are your (step)parents, and you should accept invitations to visit and make opportunities to do so.

- Reacting childishly and selfishly by refusing to visit because of where they live may cause them and you undue heartache, which is probably not your desired outcome. Show respect by calling before visiting and knocking on the door before entering.

- If family photos or other gifts to your parents are returned to you, accept them graciously. Think through the behavior rationally and recognize that it may simply be due to a different style of decorating. Continue to give your parents pictures and drawings of grandchildren if that is something you do.

- Whatever happens with other personal possessions or heirlooms, consider your reactions and the intent

144

behind the decision. If you desire specific items, discuss it maturely and rationally with your parent.

- Avoid making assumptions of your parent and stepparent's financial position and decisions. Help them if the need arises and you are financially able to do so.

- Accept the fact that Mom or Dad's and your stepparent's financial assets belong to them. They can allocate them however they choose. Encourage them to have separate wills and to put other legal documents in order to avoid probate and to minimize family squabbles. If there is an inheritance and you are included in the will, be grateful for whatever your parent does for you. Allow for your parent's marriage to evolve and expect financial changes from time to time. Placing the emphasis on the relationship rather than on an inheritance helps you to maintain proper perspective of financial decisions and your reactions.

- When it comes to issues of major concern, consult a lawyer in your area to learn the laws of your state and to protect your parent and to be aware of your legal rights.

CHAPTER 8

"But We've Always Spent the Holidays at Your House!"

*"The melding of two families' traditions into the new family's
tradition is especially difficult during the holidays. Most of the
fondest memories we and our children hold are of family
holiday times. Unfortunately, in the blended family, the fond
memories and traditions can drive wedges if not
handled thoughtfully and carefully."*

—Terri Clark

Holidays, special events, and family traditions provide many opportunities to celebrate and recognize those you love. Who doesn't remember a family treasure—the angel at the top of the tree, the silver menorah, or the antique cake stand that was only brought out and used on birthdays? These traditions may be foreign to your stepparent, but they give you a sense of security, stability, strength, and family unity. You could always count on them being part of your holiday or birthday celebration. Now you're no longer sure what you can count on.

Family Traditions

Traditions help family members develop a sense of belonging. Inclusion in traditions that are unique to the family helps both parents and children separate themselves from other families. Traditions are statements to the world and to the insiders that we belong to this unique group called "our family." With the advent of your parent's remarriage, your family is not clearly defined. Your traditions may clash with your stepparent's traditions. Family boundaries may be torn down to be rebuilt in a new configuration. These changes typically upset your sense of belonging and identity, but if you are flexible, you can join in new or modified traditions and eventually return to a feeling of secure belonging.

Specific customs, traditions, and rituals recognize a family's heritage, connecting them to their ancestors and bridging the gap between past and present. Rather than bridging the gap after the death of your parent or divorce, you may feel like the chasm has widened. Or you may experience culture shock as Mom or Dad changes some of the rituals you've known and grown accustomed to your entire life. You might be left out of some celebrations altogether.

As holidays approach, you wonder what will change and what will stay the same. This may be the initiative versus guilt stage of social development. Rather than hanging on the fringes, fearful of your beloved family tradition of baking cookies being replaced with decorating a gingerbread house, take the initiative of hosting the tradition in your home, then cooperate by joining in the customs of your stepparent. As an adult, you are old enough to understand that what's important is spending time together creating memories, not necessarily the activity. How do you decide which traditions are worth perpetuating to make memories?

Consider all of the traditions that your family practices:

- Why you do each of them?
- Which are most important to you?
- Which traditions have lost their meaning, and may be omitted?

You may have few traditions left on your list, but the ones you keep will be most dear to you and create a feeling of continuity linking you to your past. Bear in mind that your stepparent is part of this new family. Accept responsibility for including him or her in your customs to instill a feeling of belonging.

Family traditions usually involve beliefs, customs, and meaning. Traditions are repeated on a regular basis—daily, monthly, or annually. They include what families do to celebrate holidays and birthdays, but they are not limited to those. Reunions, vacations, religious services, or any number of other activities identify your family and offer enjoyment.

Children anticipate annual customs and quickly remind parents when they are forgotten. Even as an adult, you probably still look forward to some of the traditions begun when you were a child, such as a family night movie with popcorn, Sunday evening ice cream sundaes, summer family Olympics, or a birthday treasure hunt. You feel comfortable with the familiar activities that you know and love. Continuing family traditions and including your stepparent underscores the importance of the extended family.

Steve used one family tradition in particular to get better acquainted with his stepfather. "We've gone on quite a few trips together. My mom always liked to take trips with our family, so the adults in the family went on a cruise together. Another time, all thirteen of us, including grandchildren, went to Disneyland. Trips are a tradition for us. We've had family dinners, picnics, holiday parties, and family home evenings as a group. We socialize a great deal."

149

A **Parent's** Perspective

Ruth said Dave had "quite an adjustment" to make because he had lived alone quite a long time before they were married. "My family holds monthly birthday parties recognizing everyone with a birthday that month. We celebrate Mother's Day and Father's Day together and have a big Thanksgiving dinner. We included Dave before we married and continued after we married, and he fit right in." Ruth's family made Dave feel welcome. "It didn't seem like I was moving into a stranger's house. It seemed like I was moving where I belonged," said Dave.

Some families write their own family newsletters in order to stay connected. While Nick's first wife was alive, she wrote a weekly newsletter that went to each of their nine children. "My wife called every child sometime during the week. Monday morning she wrote a letter for the children," said Nick. Every week each of their nine children received information about everyone in the family. After his wife died, two of Nick's sons tried to continue the tradition but found it difficult with their many other responsibilities. When Nick remarried, the boys asked Mary to continue the family tradition. Mary was happy to do it, and now she includes information about her four children. "They are all in the family," said Mary. "They all receive a letter, so everybody is in contact." Mary's newsletter helped her children and Nick's children get to know each other. Everyone looks forward to the week's news and treasures the newsletter as part of their family history.

New Traditions

Yours, mine, and ours may be a good compromise in blending adult families. Keep what traditions you most value, adopt favorable customs of your stepparent, and create new ones. In this way, you maintain family security, promote acceptance of your stepparent, and create new boundaries defining your new family unit.

When they married, Neal had four married children and Anne had three dependent children. They wanted to blend their families, and they understood the importance of tradition to a family. They came up with an idea for a family Christmas party to bring everyone together, and the party soon became an annual tradition. "All of our family attends and brings their children and their friends," said Anne. "We did it at our home until the party got too big. Now we do it at the church. Everyone has a good time." Neal's son was initially uncomfortable with blended family functions, but over the years, he softened and now participates in more family activities. The togetherness of the new family tradition helped most of Neal's and Anne's children think of themselves as one big family. Now their grandchildren look forward to the Christmas party with the same excitement.

Lori's daughter introduced a new tradition to their family. Her son-in-law grew up never leaving the house without giving his parents a hug if they were home. He carries the tradition on in his family and shared it with Lori. "Our family was not physical in our demonstration of love, but I like this tradition. It adds warmth to our interactions," Lori said.

Perhaps your family was not demonstrative, and now you have a stepmother that hugs everyone. You may be uncomfortable with your space being invaded. Be willing to give it a try. You may find that a hug is comforting and reassuring. You may have a new tradition. Use your imagination to come up with rituals to define your new family. It could be a family cheer chanted whenever you get together or a ritual greeting or farewell. It could be a favorite drink or dessert served at dinners, a specific entrée prepared the same day of the month, a game night, or the same birthday or holiday gift such as nuts, cookies, or a doll. Traditions don't have to be expensive or extravagant or affiliated with a holiday, but rather unite you as a family.

Holidays

Holidays are times to celebrate. For children, they represent a day out of school. Maybe you look forward to a day off of work. Everyone has a favorite holiday. Perhaps it is partying to ring in the New Year, the annual Easter egg hunt, the parade and fireworks on the Fourth of July, dressing up for Halloween, or the special traditions of Hanukkah or Christmas. Holidays can be fun, joyous, and filled with laughter and togetherness, or they can be some of the most stress-filled times of the year. Scheduling can be difficult if families are large. Add to the mix stepsiblings and their families, and it is next to impossible trying to work with everyone's schedule.

Your attitude and actions will go a long way in determining what sort of celebration your family enjoys. Careful attention must be given to meld families rather than driving a wedge between them. Interfaith marriages may present sticky issues. "Instead of seeing this as a dilemma (wondering how to choose between the two religions), view this as an opportunity to blend each side of the family's customs," writes Paula Court of NYMetroParents.com.

Acceptance and tolerance of a stepparent, in general, is an important lesson to teach children. Mike extends invitations to his father and stepmother to join his family's activities on special occasions, birthdays, Christmas, and Thanksgiving. "The most important thing we've done is to include them in special occasions," he said.

Holidays have opened up a new relationship for Mike and his father, too. "Growing up, I can't remember my dad playing a board game with us," said Mike. "At Thanksgiving he's played games with us for the past few years. It has helped our relationship."

Gift Giving

Not every holiday requires that gifts be exchanged, but they can provide another way to recognize and welcome your stepparent into the family. Don't choose gifts because you think you'll get something in return. Give a gift freely with love and without ulterior motives.

Steve appreciated a gift to his family from his stepfather. "My mom is big on gift giving, so she would always take care of the gifts for our family. This last Christmas, Nolan actually chose gifts for our family. It impressed me that he would go out of his way to develop the relationship." For Steve, the gift represented his stepfather's desire to strengthen family ties.

Gift giving, like all other situations, may not turn out how you want it to. Bonnie and her brothers spent time discussing what gifts to give to their new stepmother. They pooled their money to buy her a breadmaker she mentioned she would like. She didn't express any appreciation, and she used it only twice, then placed it in a cupboard. Their stepmother made no effort to give them gifts until they married, then she gave couple gifts more out of obligation rather than sincere kindness, Bonnie felt. After many attempts to welcome their stepmother and to show their acceptance through thoughtful gifts, Bonnie said, "It's hurtful when the gifts aren't appreciated. Because of her reaction, we kind of do a mad scramble the night before. You don't feel like spending time finding something this person will love the very most. We are still trying but halfheartedly."

Part of the joy of gift giving is in witnessing the recipient's pleasure. You want to select something in the perfect color, shape, or size that will delight the individual. When the recipient opens the package, his or her facial expression reveals how well you have chosen the right gift and is often your reward for your invested time, energy, and money.

Special Events

"Learn to enjoy every minute of your life....
Every minute should be ... savored."
—Earl Nightingale

Shared memories are a hallmark of communities and of families. Spending time together on holidays, special occasions, or just because is one of the most common ways that families create and nurture these special memories. Some of our warmest recollections feature special times when all of the family convened for food, gifts, and conversation. Your parent's remarriage offers an opportunity to support one another by participating in special events.

Simply by attending the activities of various family members, you acknowledge each individual's significance. If you have a typical family life, you take children to lessons and practices and attend their games, plays, and recitals. This is part of being a parent and shows your care for your children and your desire to encourage their endeavors. Your parent and stepparent can't attend your family's activities if they are unaware of them. Make sure you let them know about the special events coming up.

Sandy appreciates her mother and stepfather's support: "My dad was a loner. He rarely attended our activities. During the first year of my mom's remarriage, Dean supported my children and me more than my dad did his whole life. Dean attended everything, whether it was for my children or something special for me. I sang in a Christmas choir for several years and

Dean was always there listening with my mom. Dean supports whatever we do as a family, whether it's a ballgame, graduation, or religious function."

Sandy has also done her own part to maintain the family get-togethers. When her siblings got married and had families of their own, the large family gatherings tapered off. "We used to get together all the time," she said. "I wanted to stay closer. We have had activities with just the adult kids, their spouses, Mom, and Dean. We have dinner, game nights, or attend a comedy club all together. We have a lot of fun."

A **Stepparent's** Perspective
Anne and Neal attend or help on many special occasions. "We visit Neal's grandchildren whenever a new baby is born," said Anne. "We've been involved in grandchildren's weddings by helping to set up and take down decorations. When children or grandchildren move into a new house, we go see their new home. We're involved in their lives. That is how we pull our families together and help them know we have an interest in them."

It only takes one person to recognize that something is missing in the family relationship and take the initiative to plan an activity. That person can be you. Sandy accepted the responsibility of helping her family stay close by organizing outings. You can start with something simple and enlist the help of others to coordinate more complicated activities.

Trudie takes the initiative in her family. "Families need to communicate and spend time together to strengthen bonds. Someone needs to take the initiative to get the family together. If no one else does it, it might as well be me," she said. Trudie initiated a family barbecue and kickball game. "No one kept score," she said. "The enjoyment came from being together and having fun. I planned two or three other family activities, then my siblings planned some."

The birth of a baby, a wedding, and moving into a new home are all exciting milestones. Sharing these events with others only increases the joy. Such special events provide pleasurable opportunities to help a new mother, plan a wedding, or give a housewarming gift.

Stepparents' Birthdays

The young want to grow up and the old want to stay young. Not everyone wants to be reminded of his or her age, but most people appreciate being the guest of honor on one day a year. Family traditions vary. Some let birthdays slip by virtually unnoticed, while others use them as opportunities for big productions. Steve said, "My stepfather, Nolan, said that he never had a party before joining our family. It's the nature of our family to celebrate birthdays."

Celebrating a birthday gives the guest of honor personal attention and recognition. Birthday dinners or parties require planning and coordination, but they are wonderful gestures that can make a stepparent feel a true part of your family. Sandy's family uses her stepfather's birthday as a time to celebrate. "One year we gave Dean a surprise birthday party. He was very appreciative and became emotional," said Sandy.

Nick's daughter, Kristen, threw a surprise seventieth birthday party for her new stepmother. "I was absolutely floored," said Mary. "All nine of Nick's kids came from various parts of the country." Mary's joy was evident as she remembered receiving so much kindness and attention.

Mary enjoyed the surprise party, but be aware that not everyone likes surprises! It would be wise to check with your parent first. The same holds true for unexpected visits. Your parent and stepparent may not tell you about plans they have, so you may arrive to find an empty house. Let your parent and stepparent know about your family birthday plans so you don't experience the situation that happened to Trudie. Her father and stepmother came to her home expecting a birthday party, only to find no one there. "Quite often, we have a family activity for our birthdays. It would be nice if my dad and his wife could join us, but my dad doesn't even call us to see if we have plans." Trudie acknowledged that she should be more proactive in the future and keep her family apprised of her plans.

Your parent and stepparent don't want to intrude, but they probably would like to be invited. Remember that the greatest gift is making someone feel accepted and loved as a member of the family.

Small Gestures Speak Volumes

Think back to a time when someone complimented you on a job well done, remembered your birthday, encouraged you on a project, or called just to say hello. Each of these gestures, although small, meant something to you. Small acts like these touch your heart and linger in your memory. They cost next to nothing, yet they accomplish their goal of motivating you or lifting your spirits.

Remembering your stepparent's birthday with a small token is fairly easy to do. A phone call, card, inexpensive gift, even a heartfelt hug or smile—for any occasion or no occasion—welcomes your stepparent as a member of your family. These are acts that would brighten anyone's day and inspire reciprocal behavior. Such small, seemingly insignificant gestures can make a big difference in your relationship with your stepparent.

Of all the special occasions in the year, Father's Day and Mother's Day are liable to be most awkward at first. You may feel uncomfortable sending a card to someone who isn't your parent, thinking that it somehow diminishes the role of your absent parent. However, acknowledging a stepparent on these special days is another way to show your acceptance of him or her as your parent's spouse.

A Stepparent's Perspective

Anne didn't expect anything from her stepdaughters, especially since they had all grown up as friends. "Since we are the same age, I wouldn't even expect a Mother's Day card or gift," said Anne. But they surprised her with gifts on Mother's Day as well as birthday gifts. "I'm honored Neal's daughters think of me in a special way, as the matriarch of the family, as their dad's partner," said Anne. "They could just think of me as someone their own age. Acknowledging me on Mother's Day is special."

Sandy recognized Dean on special days by giving him a card: "I bought cards that say 'Wonderful Stepdad.' I've never gotten to the point where I can just call him my dad." Sandy appreciates Dean as a member of their family and wants him to know it.

After Diane decided to try harder to have a relationship with her stepfather, she still struggled with mixed emotions on holidays. "I had my kids call and wish Jim a happy Father's Day," said Diane. "My mother said, 'You are the only one of my kids who has called.' I think she wishes that all of us thought of Jim in an endearing way." You may not yet feel particularly close to your stepparent, but acknowledging him or her on Mother's Day or Father's Day is a step in the right direction. Your parent will feel your support. There is never a bad time to value, honor, or be thoughtful of others.

Be Grateful

*"Gratitude unlocks the fullness of life. It turns what we have
into enough, and more. It turns denial into acceptance,
chaos to order, confusion to clarity . . . a stranger into a friend.
Gratitude makes sense of our past, brings peace for today,
and creates a vision for tomorrow."*
—*Melody Beattie*

Do you remember a time when someone thanked you or expressed appreciation for something you did? Remember your feeling of being acknowledged? A simple thank-you lets friends know that you appreciate what they have done for you. Expressing gratitude is another simple gesture that speaks volumes. Acknowledging kindnesses strengthens friendships. Whenever your stepparent does a kind act for you, be quick to express appreciation to bolster your relationship.

The surprise birthday party Sandy and her siblings gave their stepdad brought tears to his eyes. Sandy said Dean mentioned his appreciation many times to her mother. Sandy experienced joy in doing something that obviously gave him pleasure.

Steve enjoys an enriching relationship with his stepfather. They are quick to express appreciation for presents and gifts of time and service. Steve said, "My stepfather is very appreciative, and I think our family is relatively appreciative. We express gratitude readily and show affection easily." Steve's family cheerfully gives each other material gifts, which demonstrates their generous nature. Their quickness to say thank you acknowledges the effort, sacrifice, and generosity of the giver. Expressions of appreciation to your parent and stepparent indicate your desire to maintain and build upon your friendship. Gratitude communicates acceptance, fosters love, and encourages continued giving (not bad rewards for something that costs so little). Acknowledging kind acts of stepparents opens your eyes to the support and love being offered.

Sandy and Steve have a vision of continued love and acceptance. The fullness of life continues to unfold for them as they exchange many different types of gifts with their stepparent. They enjoy the gift of friendship, as gratitude is quickly and sincerely expressed.

On the other hand, ingratitude stunts or even deteriorates relationships. After their stepmother's repeated ingratitude, Bonnie and her brothers now make halfhearted attempts of gift giving and offering help: "The need for us to be included kind of died out when we realized it wasn't that important to her. You can only take so much rejection; eventually you put up a defense. You wonder what you're doing wrong."

This ingratitude made Bonnie and her brothers feel rejected. Their stepmother remains a stranger in the sense that they interact only because she is married to their father. Yet they continue to offer her acceptance by visiting her in the hospital, offering their services, and giving her gifts. A simple "thank you" would mean so much to them and make them feel accepted in return.

Take the Initiative

> *"We can let circumstances rule us, or we can take charge*
> *and rule our lives from within."*
> —*Earl Nightingale*

You can allow others to control your relationships, or you can take charge and craft them as you desire. After your mom or dad remarries, her or his priorities change. As parents age, their energy diminishes. They may no longer plan family interactions as they once did. Your life may seem a bit empty without the annual family reunion or the monthly family dinner. To maintain or improve your relationships with your parent and stepparent, initiate opportunities to be together. If you wait for them to make the first move, family togetherness may never happen.

Diane recognizes that her mother is preoccupied with her husband and their activities, yet she desires to have her mom be part of her family. Diane initiates phone calls to keep her mother informed of her family's activities. Diane encourages her children to share things with their grandmother. For example, Diane said, "The first time my daughter went potty on the toilet, I said, 'Let's call Grandma and tell her.' My daughter would not call or initiate it; I have to help that along." Diane is nurturing the relationship between her daughter and her mother. She is also aware of her stepfather's financial concerns, so she sends her mother calling cards to phone her children and grandchildren. Diane's initiatives maintain harmony with her stepfather and foster her relationship with her mother.

Sandy's family has also benefited from her initiative. As her siblings married and became involved and busy with their children's activities, Sandy felt the desire to stay close to them. She described her action: "We hadn't been doing anything together as a family. As our children have matured, we've gone separate directions. I plan the activity because nobody else will. Coordinating the schedules of six couples is difficult, so we have whoever can come." Sandy's initiative maintains family unity by consistently spending time together. If you feel something is missing in your family relationships, accept the responsibility of organizing a dinner or other activity.

It is unreasonable to expect parents to always initiate contact with you, especially if they are living on a limited budget. One of Katie's sisters complained that their dad wasn't calling very often. Rather than letting it bother her, Katie initiates phone calls to maintain contact. "Dad's never been one to call much," said Katie. "I'm usually the one making the phone calls. Dad finally got a cell phone and doesn't get charged long distance, so that has helped since he doesn't have a lot of money." Katie recognizes the financial limitations of her father and his wife, and she takes the initiative to maintain contact.

Various reasons such as health, finances, or time may inhibit your parent and stepparent from keeping in touch with you. It doesn't mean they don't want contact. Katie and Diane recognized some of those inhibitions and overcame them by making wise choices in initiating the phone calls or sending a calling card. Love finds a way to express itself when you are willing to act.

Raising a family consumes your time and requires effort and coordination. Focusing on your immediate family leaves little time for socializing, even with your parent and his or her spouse. However, you may sense that something is missing in your life. Activities with Mom or Dad, your stepparent, and extended family unify and enrich your life; they are worth the effort required to coordinate them.

Initiative Versus Guilt

During the initiative versus guilt stage of social-emotional development, children learn to cooperate with others at times being the leader and at other times content to follow. Some children in this phase of life cling to Mom or Dad. They are fearful and tend to hang on the fringes of group activities, thereby inhibiting their ability to be part of the group. When it comes to holiday celebrations or family traditions, uncertainty about changing family boundaries may cause you to stand back. You're not sure whether you should follow your parent in creating new traditions or assume the role of leader in continuing long-established family rituals. This is a time to exercise your initiative and do both. Take the lead and plan a tradition important to you that may be overlooked, but also be flexible and participate in family customs that may be new. Initiate activities that you feel will strengthen family bonds, and include rather than exclude your new stepparent.

Take Action

The first step is always the hardest. Each succeeding step becomes progressively easier. Decide what is most comfortable for you with traditions, holidays, and special events. One option is to invite Mom or Dad and your stepparent to join your family for a special dinner. Another approach would be sending a card or calling to say happy Father's Day or Mother's Day. If your relationship is strained and both of those feel awkward, have your children call. Whose heart wouldn't melt by hearing a child say, "Hi, Grandma. I hope you're having a good day." Any and all of these represent your desire and willingness to recognize your stepparent as Mom or Dad's spouse.

Here is an example of taking action with family traditions. Perhaps your family has a big feast with traditional foods to celebrate New Year's Eve, then relaxes and watches football games New Year's Day at Mom and Dad's home. Enter a stepparent who foregoes late-night partying and opts for a simple New Year's Day dinner after a day on the ski slopes or at the beach. That is about as opposite as you can get. How do you compromise?

Begin with the questions at the beginning of the chapter:

- Why am I doing this? (Are you doing it for togetherness or simply because everyone else is partying on that day?)
- Are these traditions important to me? (Is it the traditional foods, the partying, watching the games, or being at Mom and Dad's home? Perhaps you'd rather be active

outside, while your stepdad prefers to be a couch potato during football games.)

➤ Does it accomplish something worthwhile or has it lost its meaning? (Time together is worthwhile, but could you be together doing something else more meaningful?)

After answering these questions, you are better equipped to make decisions. You could host the party at your place, and that way Mom or Dad and your stepparent could leave at their leisure. If they choose not to attend the party, do something together the following day. Record the football games to watch at another time and have a barbecue on the beach instead. Or if you have snow, go sledding or build a snowman. Or put a puzzle together while you watch the football game—something totally new for both families. You could decide to respect each other's traditions and celebrate separately with no hard feelings.

This scenario gives you an idea of how to use the questions to determine what traditions and rituals are most important to you, take into consideration other family members, and define your family.

Possible Scenario

You look forward to certain family traditions that Mom or Dad has always planned. As the time for a favorite tradition approaches, you've heard nothing about it. Rather than missing it, you decide to ask Dad what's happening.

Child: Hey, Dad. I haven't heard from you yet about our Fourth of July barbecue. Are we still having it?

Parent: We didn't know if anyone would be interested anymore.

Child: Are you kidding? Of course, we are. The barbecue and watching the community fireworks in the evening have been our tradition since I was little. If you can't host it, we'll host it at our house.

Parent: Son, I think it might be a good idea for you to host it, and I'll try to talk my wife into attending.

The Heart of the Matter

Traditions, customs, rituals, regardless of what you call them, their purpose is the same—to define your family by determining boundaries that separate your family from others; to help each family member identify with the family as a unique unit; to create a feeling of continuity, comfort, and security; to give meaning to holidays; to provide a sense of belonging; to celebrate your family's uniqueness; to bond you together. Continue your favorite traditions and be willing to embrace new ones as you redefine your family.

- Accept your stepparent's invitations to participate in old or new family traditions. Take your turn as planner or host. Incorporate new traditions into the stepfamily. Find activities that you can incorporate into family traditions, such as playing and enjoying music together.
- Remember your stepparent on holidays. If you're uncomfortable sending Mother's Day or Father's Day cards, have your children send one as a way to ease into the habit.
- Attend special events that are important to your parent and stepparent. Be sure to invite them to help and be part of your family's important functions, from religious ceremonies to recitals. Invite your parent and stepparent to family birthday parties. Discuss family birthday plans with them. Plan a birthday party for your stepparent.

- ☙ A simple gift, phone call, or card speaks volumes. Be generous in your appreciation of material gifts, emotional gifts, and gifts of time. Be quick to say thank you and to acknowledge the sacrifices and efforts of your stepparent to do something nice for you.

- ☙ Don't wait for your mom or dad to plan activities as they did before they remarried. You are old enough to plan family activities; take the initiative and do it. Accommodate as many schedules as possible, then enjoy being together. Then plan another one. Watch family harmony increase.

CHAPTER 9

"Don't Discipline My Children"

*"One of the nicest things that has ever happened to me
in my life is Emma's grandchildren."*

—Ron Griggs

S tep-grandparents can be wonderful influences on grandchildren, especially when parents help create an attitude that this new grandparent is an addition, not a replacement.

Grandchildren play a unique role in any family, but in mature stepfamilies they provide a wonderful avenue for embracing a new step-grandparent. Naturally full of unconditional love, young children present a way to ease into stepfamily relationships. Children climb onto their step-grandparents' laps, give them hugs and kisses, and bask in the attention showered upon them. Children want to do nice things for their grandparents, like drawing a picture for them, inviting them to dinner, or calling to talk to them. These behaviors say, "I love you. I want to be part of your life." Encourage these behaviors in your children to welcome and love your new stepparent.

Talk with your children regardless of their ages. Before the wedding, let them know that their grandma or grandpa will be marrying someone else, so they will have another grandma or grandpa to love them. Explain that some things may be different, such as visiting them at a different house. Children oftentimes follow your example as the parent, so speak kindly of your parent and stepparent.

In your relationship with Mom or Dad and his or her new spouse, issues arise concerning your children that you are wise to consider. For example, how do you want your children to address their new grandparent? Discipline isn't an issue for you as an adult, but it is for your children. What role do you want your stepparent to play in your children's lives? Grandparents can be a great blessing in grandchildren's lives, acting as playmate, confidante, mentor, teacher, and cheerleader. If one of your parents passed away, a step-grandparent could fill that role for your children. Or your children could fill a void in your stepparent's life if he or she doesn't have children or grandchildren. As is true with previously discussed issues, the choice is yours. Familiarity with the consequences helps when making a decision. Here are examples of what others have done.

Addressing a Step-Grandparent

Addressing step-grandparents with respect is just as important for your children as it is for you. Young children find it easy to adopt another grandma or grandpa who loves them and wants to be part of their life. How fortunate for your children to have another person to love them! You can influence your young children by referring to your stepparent as Grandma, Grandpa, or other appropriate name. Some children take matters into their own hands and decide what to call them. After my dad's remarriage, my seven-year-old daughter asked my stepmother, "Is it all right if I call you Grandma Wilma?" My stepmother smiled as she embraced my daughter and replied, "That would be just fine." Such instances inspire a feeling of family belonging, love, and acceptance.

On the other hand, older children and teenagers may feel uncomfortable calling them Grandma or Grandpa. My ten-year-old son said to me, "Mom, she's not my grandma, so I don't think I should call her Grandma. Do I have to?" I reassured him that he didn't have to call her Grandma. Some older children change once they adjust to the new grandparent and naturally use an endearing title. Your attitude toward your stepparent and the marriage may also affect your children. Be careful and speak respectfully of your stepparent, and set a good example.

A **Stepparent's** Perspective

Marie is the only grandmother that her step-grandchildren know, so it is easy for them to call her Grandma. "At first my step-grandchildren, who were young, referred to me as Marie, then bit by bit the grandma came through. I am Grandma to them. My grandchildren, who were older, call my husband Grandpa John."

Steve's children were born after their maternal grandmother remarried, but they knew and remembered their paternal grandfather and were teenagers when Steve's mother remarried. "We haven't gotten to the point where my kids call Nolan Grandpa. It is different with my wife's mother and her husband. The only maternal grandpa that our kids have known is my wife's stepfather, and they call him Grandpa D. Our children are old enough that I can't imagine them calling Nolan Grandpa N."

Diane shared how her children address their step-grand-father: "Since my father died before my children were born, they didn't know my dad. My stepfather's name is Jim, and so my children call him Papa Jim." If you have already adapted to your parent's new marital situation before your children are born, referring to your stepparent as Grandma or Grandpa seems natural.

Of course, Mom or Dad is anxious for his or her new spouse to be accepted by the family and may inadvertently make reference to a new grandma or grandpa, much to your chagrin. Sarah described her reaction to this situation: "Both of my parents really encouraged my children to call their spouse Grandma and Grandpa. Yet ironically it backfired. To call their spouse Grandma or Grandpa, which to me is a term of endearment, is almost offensive when they are not fulfilling that role. My parents' efforts had the opposite effect—they were trying to encourage inclusion and it made me bristle. She is not their grandma; he is not their grandpa. It would make a difference if the grandparent really made an effort to fill that role and act like a grandparent."

Sarah's story illustrates some adult children's uneasiness with inappropriate coercion to have them or their children use titles they are uncomfortable with (which is not the desired intent). You may be struggling with the marriage, and to have a term of endearment forced upon you or your children adds insult to injury. Most adult children appreciate the efforts of parents and stepparents to love, support, and encourage their small or adolescent children. A stepparent who ignores your children or treats them less favorably than his or her own grandchildren causes offense. You may feel like limiting your interaction with them. Yet, when a stepparent assumes the role of a grandparent and loves your children, you are more likely to refer to her or him as Grandma or Grandpa.

What You Can Do

In case of divorce, a parent might show opposition to your children calling a stranger "Grandma." Certainly, you don't want to cause offense, but you also want Dad's new wife to feel accepted. Circumstances may not be conducive to discussing the issue together, but you can discuss it with each one individually. Let your mother or father know you don't want to hurt her or his feelings but you also want to be respectful to your stepparent. Perhaps you could agree on another name, such as Nana, Abuela, or Grammy. You could let your children decide what makes them comfortable.

Discipline

Depending on the ages of your children, they may stay with their (step)-grandparents on occasion and need to be disciplined. At the very least, your children will visit Grandma and Grandpa with you and may require discipline. Different rules may apply in their home than what you and your children are accustomed to. They may have fragile or valuable trinkets not meant for little hands. Problems could arise if your stepparent disciplines your children, especially if you are present. Discuss your parenting philosophy with your parent and stepparent. Ask if they have special rules in their home that they would like your children to observe. Notice fragile or valuable items that might be tempting to little hands. It might be best to place them out of reach while you are visiting. Respect the rules and possessions in your parent's home by maintaining proper discipline of your children. Don't be annoyed if your stepparent corrects your children when you have failed to do so and the situation merits reproof.

Melanie's stepfather, Dan, is the only grandfather from her side that her children have known, so it felt natural for Dan to discipline when appropriate. Melanie said, "A few times my stepfather has gotten upset with my kids, but he's human. Dan has never disciplined our children harshly or said anything rude to them. He's always been very supportive, kind, generous, and wonderful." More than likely, you've been irritated or frustrated with your children. Children warrant correction from time to time. Melanie was not offended when Dan corrected her children, especially when it was done in a loving manner.

Steve said, "I think when my stepfather makes mistakes is when he tries to be more of a parent and a disciplinarian and take the role of correcting. My sister has complained a little bit about it. Her family is with Mom and Nolan more often than my family. It is a mistake for step-grandparents to assume the role of disciplinarian unless they've been part of the family for a long period of time."

Your child-rearing philosophy may be different from your parent's, which may be different from your stepparent's. A behavior that you find inappropriate may be something your parent or stepparent just ignores, or vice versa. They may discipline your child for something that is common behavior in your home. For example, your children may be allowed to prepare their own breakfast or lunch or to pour themselves a glass of milk without your help, while at Grandma or Grandpa's house that behavior may be unacceptable. Imagine how confusing that would be for a child! Double standards occur frequently throughout life, but try explaining that to a four-year-old. Yet, sometimes it is amazing what children understand when we take the time to teach them.

Grandparent Role

Having raised a family, grandparents understand a few things about children. They love their grandchildren and most enjoy spending time with grandchildren without the challenge of being the primary caregiver or disciplinarian. It is natural to love small children and for them to return the love. For this reason it may appear easier for your stepparent to assume the role of a grandparent. Grandparents play a unique role in the lives of their grandchildren. For the young ones, a grandparent is often a playmate or hero. Moving into adolescence a grandparent becomes a mentor. During the teenage years and adulthood a grandparent becomes a role model, a living example of someone who has endured the vicissitudes of life while maintaining a healthy outlook. At every age, a grandparent is often a confidante and nurturer. Grandparents are often the storytellers who pass on values from previous generations and connect grandchildren with their heritage. What better friend could you desire for your children? Be willing to facilitate a relationship between your children and your stepparent.

Having no children of his own, Dave was delighted to be a grandfather and enjoyed the title. He adapted easily to sitting on the floor playing games with his little grandchildren. He took his grandchildren fishing. He talked with them and did things with them that they enjoyed doing. The grandchildren knew Dave loved them because he spent time with them doing what they liked. Who benefited? Everyone. Dave was thrilled to have all these grandchildren who loved him. The children benefited from having a playmate, a teacher, a confidante. The parents benefited by having another person in the lives of their children who loved them unconditionally and offered a positive role model.

Grandparents show love by remembering birthdays and holidays, attending activities and special events when possible, and learning of grandchildren's interests, hobbies, schoolwork, etc. Younger grandchildren, who may not know or remember a deceased grandparent, enjoy the attention of any grandparent without differentiating between step or natural grandparent.

Marie has treated her step-grandchildren as her own; hence she loves them as her own. And they love her. While looking through a photo album with her young grandson, Marie pointed to a picture of his deceased grandmother and said, "Oh, look, there is your real grandma." She said he quickly replied, "No, it isn't. You're my real grandma." That is unadulterated love and loyalty, pure and simple.

Marie has been and continues to be actively involved in her grandchildren's lives: "I've taught my granddaughters how to sew. We go horseback riding together. I phone my grandchildren a lot. I send them little notes on e-mail, just exactly the same as if they had been born through my blood. I have bent over backwards to be Grandma to them in every way, exactly as I behave with my own grandchildren. I love those little kids dearly, and they are a part of my life. Because of that we have a very good relationship, but I have worked at it."

Marie is another example of a grandparent who has nurtured her relationships with grandchildren as they grew and matured. She utilized her time with them during visits to share her talents by teaching them. She communicates regularly with them to remain a vital part of their lives. Marie enjoys being a grandma and recognizes her influence with her grandchildren without differentiating between natural and step. Her desire to bless their lives is a natural outpouring of her love for them. In return her grandchildren love her. Marie fulfills the role of grandma. She and her grandchildren have truly blessed each other's lives.

Fostering Relationships

Some grandparents easily initiate interaction with grand-children, playing with them, talking to them, and asking about their favorite toys and activities. They take teenagers shopping or to a movie. They create a loving bond. Other grandparents find it challenging to interact with grandchildren. They are willing but may have forgotten how to play with children or how to interact with teenagers. Being a step-grandparent may cause inhibitions in developing relationships with step-grandchildren. Distance may exacerbate these problems. Yet you want your children to know, love, and enjoy their grand-parents. Adult children to the rescue! That's you. It's okay to offer suggestions of what to do, of activities to engage in, or conversations to pursue. A child's invitation to play softens grandparents' hearts and reminds them of what children enjoy doing. Grandparents are usually quick to accept the invitation and have fun engaging in child's play.

Diane's mother, Ginny, raised seven children, and Diane remembers the fun times and activities she had with her mom. During visits Ginny spends most of her time interacting with adults rather than with grandchildren. Diane initiates oppor-tunities for her children to engage their grandma: "It has been hard for me to figure out my mom. If you are not around lit-tle kids, maybe you forget how to play with them and what they enjoy. I make more of an effort to get out toys and have my children ask Grandma to play. Mom plays with them, but she doesn't think of it on her own. I'll say, 'Ask Grandma if she'll take you to the park,' or 'Take this polish to Grandma and ask her if she'll paint your toenails.' Mom does it when prompted."

A **Grandparent's** Perspective

Ruth loved Dave as a companion and appreciated his influence with her grandchildren: "Dave is really creative because he's worked with kids. Dave will spend at least half of the time with our grandkids when they come. The young grandsons want Grandpa whenever they visit. They go up to Grandpa's room or down in the family room. Dave's in there with the grandkids because he knows how to entertain them. He's filled a place in their hearts, that's for sure."

Diane continued, "I want my children to like my mom, to love her, to be glad she's their grandma, and to know she is a neat person. But they haven't been able to see my mom that much or to talk to her that much. My mom never asks to talk to my children when she's talking to me on the phone. I don't think it is a malicious thing; she just doesn't think about it. Mom sends her grandchildren birthday cards and Christmas cards but she doesn't know them." During phone calls Diane prompts her children to share experiences with their grandmother.

Retirement years provide grandparents with time to play a game with grandchildren, watch a movie together, go fishing, provide day care, or have them spend the night. These activities can help your children adopt a new grandparent. Valerie and her husband both worked when their two boys were young. Her mother and stepfather cared for them during the day. Valerie said her boys developed a special bond with her stepfather, as he took the time to play and sing with them. Neal loves to fish and has plenty of time to do it. He often takes the children or grandchildren with him, which has endeared him to them.

Since grandparents who live a distance away cannot babysit or help in other ways, they try to remember grandchildren's birthdays and special events, but sometimes they simply forget significant milestones. Some children notice their grandparents' absence or the missing card or gift. Once again, you can be the unsung hero as Richard has been on occasion. When his dad has forgotten a birthday, Richard said, "We call and remind him of special events such as a forgotten birthday. It's a big deal to the kids, not so much the money but just the expectation of having it acknowledged." Richard's father appreciates the reminder. No one is offended, but they work together adjusting to different conditions in order to maintain relationships.

Sometimes teenagers perceive grandparents as being old fogies, old-fashioned, and boring. Physical health or conditioning may prevent them from participating in physical activities, confirming the stereotype. However, many grandparents are in excellent health and physical condition. Participating in various activities not only refutes the stereotypical grandparent image, but it also keeps grandparents young at heart and connects them to their grandchildren and, therefore, to you.

Throughout their marriage Melanie's mother and stepfather, Dan, have engaged in various activities with Melanie's family. "Dan is just his personable self. He interacts with our children in conversations and he might play a game with them. He has taken them to a movie. He has always been loving and kind to our children." Melanie's teenage children want to keep in touch with their grandparents and now use modern technology to do so. "This is kind of fun. The kids have just gotten e-mail accounts. So every night they e-mail and converse with both Grandpa and Grandma." Computer-savvy grandparents stay connected with grandchildren.

Steve's stepfather, Nolan, still in good health, has snorkeled with his grandchildren, played in the swimming pool with them, and vacationed with them, creating loving bonds that connect the three generations. Old fogie? Not this grandfather. He is willing to have a good time by joining in the fun.

Lack of grandparent involvement and favoritism cause hurt feelings that may linger for years. Sarah shared her feelings of frustration with the lack of support from her father and his new wife. They married when Sarah had four small children and lived in the same town. Sarah described her situation: "I had bad health problems. I was treading water so much of the time. It was frustrating because my dad and his wife never once had our kids over to spend the night or do any grandparent thing that they did with her grandchildren. We invited them to our children's sports games. Sometimes they came but not very often."

Generativity Versus Stagnation

This phase of the relationship, connecting the generations, coincides with Erikson's generativity versus stagnation stage. Generativity deals with parenting and learning to satisfy and support the generations. Each generation—grandchildren, parents, grandparents—has its unique role to interact productively to love and support one another. Creativity and imagination create interest and enthusiasm in these relationships. Prompting children to ask a grandparent questions teaches them to value and respect their grandparents. Encouraging children to ask Grandma to paint their nails or Grandpa to play a game of chess creates a fond memory of a special time together. Sleepovers allow grandparents to dote on their grandchildren, linking their hearts as they laugh, play games, read, or make a special treat together.

Consider ways you, as a parent, can foster the relationship between your children, your mom or dad, and your stepparent. The alternative of vibrant, growing relationships is stagnation, which is void of progress and growth.

Take Action

Perhaps your situation is similar to Sarah's, where her father and stepmother had little involvement in her children's lives. Here are a few options available to you:

- Ask them if they would be willing to have your children spend the night.
- Invite them as guests of honor for "This Is Your Life." Prep your children with questions to ask. Prepare their favorite dessert. Have your children present them with a memento representing their life.
- Invite them to your children's birthday or other events.
- Find ways to involve your children in their grandparents' celebrations or important events in the grandparents' lives.

If they show no interest or desire in being grandparents, focus on nurturing relationships with other grandparents.

Possible Scenario

You and your spouse are leaving for the weekend and your mom and stepfather have agreed to take care of your children while you are gone.

Child: Mom and Jack, this is so nice of you to watch our children while we are away.

Parent: We're excited to have them.

Child: They're usually pretty good kids. Just in case you have a problem, let me share how we discipline. If they do something inappropriate or disobey, we talk to them and explain the problem. Then we tell them how we want them to behave. That is our warning to them. If they do it a second time, they receive a time-out for five minutes, after which they have to tell us what they did wrong and how they will correct it. If it happens again, they have to choose a chore to do, acceptable to us, and still tell us what they will do differently.

Parent: That sounds simple. I think we'll be okay. We have some fun activities planned.

The Heart of the Matter

Children can melt grandparents' hearts easier than anything else. Just ask any grandparent. Your parent's remarriage expands your family and brings the blessing of another grandparent. Love, rather than blood, creates ties that bind. If you are experiencing anxiety in your relationship with your stepparent, try using your children to improve the situation. It might sound selfish to "use" your children, but in stepfamily situations children often offer love and acceptance more freely than adults. This should be "one, big, happy family," and your children are part of this family too. Experience the serenity and love that comes as you bridge the generations of your family.

- Ask your stepparent how he or she would like to be addressed by your children. Teach small children to call him or her Grandpa and Grandma or another variation acceptable to your stepparent. If your teenagers are uncomfortable with using the term Grandma or Grandpa, encourage them to be respectful, and perhaps suggest an alternative appellation such as Papa Joe or Nana Jane.
- Discipline of your children may arise as an issue with your stepparent. Decide how you want to handle it when your children stay with grandparents. Discuss your discipline philosophy with grandparents, so if they are in a position

where correction is needed, they can discipline your children according to your philosophy. Be sensitive to your children's behavior when visiting grandparents. Inquire about special concerns or rules in your parent's home. It is your responsibility to teach your children to respect the rules and property of their grandparents. When present, handle any problem that arises with your children.

➤ Some step-grandparents naturally bond with grandchildren. Others need encouragement. As both the child and parent, you can facilitate the relationship by encouraging communication with grandparents in person, on the phone, or through e-mail. Make suggestions to your children of things to do with Grandma or Grandpa. Extend invitations to grandparents to attend your children's activities even when rebuffed.

CHAPTER 10

"Is It Okay to Contact My Ex-Stepmother?"

"Charity suffereth long, and is kind; charity envieth not;
charity vaunteth not itself, is not puffed up, doth not behave
itself unseemly, seeketh not her own, is not easily provoked,
thinketh no evil; rejoiceth not in iniquity, but rejoiceth
in the truth; beareth all things, believeth all things, hopeth
all things, endureth all things. Charity never faileth."
—*1 Corinthians 13:4–8*

D isaster eventually strikes every mature stepfamily. The inevitable happens—one of the spouses dies. Or the undesirable occurs—divorce (perhaps that was your desire all along). The best family infrastructure cannot prevent death, nor the best counseling circumvent divorce. Searching, without success, for a safe haven from these natural events of life, parents find themselves single and lonely yet again. Life insurance policies provide little comfort. Policies may cover burial costs and a stipend on which to live, but money can never replace the companionship of a beloved husband, wife, or parent. It is a Band-Aid that does not begin to cover the injury nor heal the pain and loneliness parents once again experience from the loss.

Afflicted with grief, you mourn the loss of your parent or cherished friend. Shock, denial, and anger visited you at least once before when you confronted your parents' breakup or the death of one you loved. Now they return to torment you again. You may want the world to stop for just a moment and acknowledge your loss. Instead, all around you life goes on, and so must you. Fortunately, you are not alone. You have your family. Families naturally turn to each other for solace in their time of loss. Love provides some comfort especially if you've taken the time to develop supportive relationships. On the other hand, if you've isolated yourself from your family, you may put forth an air of stoicism and aloofness. Internally, you may be pleading for forgiveness and to be reclaimed as a family member.

If it is your parent who died, you must decide how to interact with your stepparent and other stepfamily members. Questions abound. How much input should I have in the funeral? Should I call my stepmom? What should I say? Do I continue my relationship or break it off? Your stepparent also has decisions to make concerning association with the stepfamily. Whether interaction continues usually depends on the quality of the relationships while the marriage was intact. Unfortunately, you or your stepparent may recognize the value of your affinity too late and miss out on the love and support you could offer each other. Happily, those who developed cherished friendships continue to love and support each other during the grieving process and beyond. They have learned that family includes more than blood relatives, and these loving ties are not severed by death.

If it is your stepparent who died, questions still abound. Do I attend the funeral? How can I help Mom or Dad? Should I maintain contact with stepsiblings? The answers to these questions depend once again on your relationships during the marriage.

Divorce presents similar dilemmas. If you never liked your stepparent, you may be glad the marriage ended and you no longer need to deal with this person. But you may occasionally bump into each other. How should you react? There are instances where children like the stepparent more than their parent. What happens to their friendship? What governs your interactions? Unfortunately, there are no hard and fast rules. However, a good guideline is to be gracious and to let charity determine your behavior.

Families offer the ideal setting to develop the biblical characteristics of charity. Perhaps you've developed a few of these virtues—kindness, humility, loyalty, optimism, among others. You may still be trying to acquire some of them. You have yet another opportunity to work on them. As described in the quote at the beginning of this chapter, charity is patient in tribulation and seeks ways to make life pleasant for others. In time of death or divorce, you are there to comfort and support your parent or stepparent. Offer assistance in planning funeral arrangements. Attend the funeral. Charity is accepting your situation and improving it. You can't bring the dead back to life nor can you reinstate a dissolved marriage, but you can be a refuge by maintaining contact with your parent or stepparent, inviting her or him to your home, or visiting them. If you possess charity, you rejoice with others and are gracious in your behavior. Most of the time, you do not rejoice over a death or divorce, but rather can offer a shoulder to cry on, lend a listening ear, or give a warm embrace. You make sacrifices in order to bring joy to others and are compassionate, overlooking and forgiving errors. In time of disaster people crave any form of genuine care and concern rather than criticism or "I told you so." Sincere compassion is a pinnacle of humanity that gives giving others a reason to move forward. You look for opportunities to do what is right and good. You honor your parent or stepparent for the joy given and service rendered to his or her companion. You are honest in interactions and endure all things by putting forth your best effort. Regardless of how others treat you, you are good and kind and are rewarded with peace of mind. Charity encompasses every aspect of life, making us a better person and our family relationships more rewarding.

When disaster strikes by either death or divorce, stand ready to help and support those you love. Sometimes it takes a disaster for you to recognize how important someone is in your life and to appreciate what you no longer have. At the same time you cleave to what remains with you. Disaster has a funny way of reminding you that your family is your most precious possession. Consider how you would like to be treated by your stepparent or how you would like stepchildren to treat your parent, then behave in a mature and respectful manner.

Divorce

Marriage creates bonds—good, bad, or indifferent—tying a couple and family together. Of course, the ideal is to have a successful union and a happy family. But alas, that is not always the case. For one reason or another, marriages deteriorate. Bonds are broken and families splintered. Individuals are left to pick up the pieces of their lives the best they can. They try to make sense of the insensible. When parents divorce, children may take sides, especially when one party is obviously at fault. Family ties are reshaped and relationships reconfigured. Is divorce in a remarriage any different? In some ways it is.

Pam's second marriage lasted five years. During that time Pam and Brad developed relationships with each other's children. Pam's children got along with Brad and liked him okay until toward the end of the marriage. Pam developed health problems and her children noticed that Brad was not emotionally supportive. Following their divorce, two of Pam's four children called Brad a couple of times to let him know that they still cared for him and they appreciated what he had done for them. Pam said that she continued to talk to Brad once or twice a week on the phone until he told her he was remarried. "And that was the end of that," said Pam.

Pam continued, "I just love Brad's children. They are awesome people. I don't keep in touch with them. I probably should. I think about them. I don't know if contacting them would be appropriate. I figure, well, Brad has his life and that's okay."

During their marriage, Pam, Brad, and their children recognized and appreciated good qualities in one another. Pam enjoyed interacting with Brad's children. Pam's sons enjoyed socializing with Brad. They created some happy memories. When the marriage ended in divorce, the continued contact represented the friendship that transpired. Pam's children's occasional phone calls to Brad were gestures of kindness. Following Brad's subsequent marriage, contact ceased. Contact while Brad was single was appropriate and respectful. Brad's new spouse might feel uncomfortable with her husband talking to a former wife and stepchildren. With new bonds formed, it was time to sever old ones. Occasionally, you hear of an ex-wife and current wife who actually become friends. Relationships may continue amicably among stepchildren or with a stepparent. Since you know yourself and other key players, you are best able to decide appropriate interactions.

Prior to her marriage to Phil, Cara was not acquainted with her husband's children. "I should have taken it as a red flag," said Cara. "However, Phil spent the holidays with my family. My family knew him well. They all liked him. They thought

Phil was cute and funny and nice. He was good to me and to my children." Four months after their marriage, Cara started annulment proceedings.

During their brief marriage, Cara became acquainted with Phil's children. "Four of his five children are good kids. They are nice. To this day our relationship, whenever I see them, is nice. If my children run into Phil, they are all decent." Cara and Phil still talk on occasion. Their marriage didn't last long enough for the children to develop ties with one another, so there is no interest in pursuing relationships that never existed. Nor do Cara's children go out of their way to contact Phil. Since they live in the same vicinity, they occasionally run into each other around town. They have no animosity toward Phil's family, so it is easy for them to be friendly and cordial.

Kindness should prevail in stepfamily relationships when the marriage does not work out. Regardless of whether you are happy with the outcome, how the ex-partner treated your parent, how the other stepchildren treated you or your parent, the option is yours to choose how you will treat former family members. It is not necessary to condone any unkind behavior or to go out of your way to maintain contact, but chance meetings can still be civil.

Amanda's second marriage lasted one year. Problems arose quickly and they sought counseling but were unable to correct the problems. Amanda said, "I enjoyed Greg's children and wanted to keep in touch with one of his daughters with whom I developed a friendship quickly. After the divorce I felt that I needed to make a complete break so Greg couldn't get information about me from any of his children."

In some instances it hurts to sever a relationship. Perhaps you've developed a cherished friendship with your stepparent. You enjoyed each other's company. When the marriage ends, you may be surprised if your stepparent stops all interaction. Or you may feel that it is best to end contact. You hope that those whom you've grown to love will understand and not take it personally. You may resume contact at a later time when you are more comfortable with the situation. Even though this is an acceptable reaction, the distance between contacts may make later interaction awkward.

On occasion adult children may choose to continue a relationship with an ex-stepparent. You have probably formed many friendships throughout your life independent of your parents. It just so happens that you develop a special tie with your stepmom and resist giving it up after a divorce. Then by all means continue it. The friendship that binds you is probably based on mutual interests, service to one another, and time spent together rather than on a legal contract. Your stepmom, your friend, may appreciate remaining part of your life and your children's lives.

Death

Death of a parent or stepparent presents a different scenario.

While living in the same city as her father and his wife, Jenny, Sarah tried hard to connect to Jenny. It just did not work out. Eventually, Sarah's family moved to a different state. Sarah's father became ill and died. Sarah said, "Ironically since my dad's death, my stepmother writes me these lovely letters. 'Miss you so much. Wish you were here.' I still respond to her, but it is too late to have a relationship. Why would we have one now? It doesn't even make sense. I don't want to invest the energy or time when it wasn't important to her while he was alive. Sometimes I feel like it is just a connection with my dad to keep a relationship with me."

Sometimes opportunities present themselves only once. That includes opportunities to develop relationships. If you are estranged from your parent and stepparent during their marriage, it is highly unlikely that you would want a relationship with a stepparent following the death of your mom or dad. That opportunity is gone, regardless of how close you live to each other. All relationships require time and energy to maintain. If you already have a busy schedule, chances are remote that you would want to invest any free time in a relationship that was insignificant while your parent was alive. However, it is common courtesy to respond to a letter or other communication as Sarah did.

Max's mother, Evelyn, dated her second husband, Glen, for twenty-eight years before they married. During the courtship, Glen's children opposed marriage plans. Eventually, they came to love Evelyn. They saw how kind she was to their father throughout their courtship and their one year of marriage before their father died of cancer. Max said the stepchildren are wonderful to his mother now and occasionally the two families interact socially. Max appreciates the kindness and acceptance shown to his mother.

Some people truly are patient and long-suffering. Twenty-eight years is a long time to wait for children to sanction a parent's marriage. Imagine Max's heartache knowing that his mother could have had many years of happiness in marriage if not for the selfishness of Glen's children. Yet Max chooses to focus on how kind they treat his mother now. Yes, they made mistakes that cannot be changed, but their behavior now is wonderful. Both families enjoy the association they continue to have.

Strained Relationships

Some adults, displeased with their parent's marriage, make life unpleasant for their mom or dad and stepparent during the marriage and continue childish behavior after their parent dies. They fail to recognize the self-inflicted damage of such behavior. They cut themselves off from their parent and forego a relationship with a stepparent who may truly love their mom or dad and desire to be an addition to the family rather than a detriment. They miss out on the love and support they could both give and receive throughout the grieving process.

Jackie said that her mother's stepchildren, with one exception, were rude to her mom, Betty, throughout her marriage to their father. The stepchildren's treatment of Betty broke Jackie's heart since her mother took such good care of their father before he died. Jackie said, "One son continues to be kind to my mother while the other children are still rude."

Rudeness, the antithesis of kindness, has no place in relationships. It is demeaning to the individual and adversely affects family associations. It hampers the personal growth of the perpetrators. If you find yourself being rude to a parent or stepparent, try to take the time to realize the damage being done to yourself and so many others. Recognize that you need to re-evaluate and change your behavior. Rather than causing heartache, you could spread happiness. Take effort to correct your behavior while your parent and stepparent are here to forgive you.

Jake lamented the lost relationship with his dad, who focused his attention on his new wife and her daughters. His dad suffers from cancer with little time to live. Jake uses his emotional pain as a crutch to find excuses for not visiting his dad. Tears came to Jake's eyes as he vocalized his fear of his father's death before mending their relationship. If you find yourself in a similar situation, stop procrastinating. Find the strength and determination to overcome pain, pride, fear, or whatever else may be holding you back from healing a strained relationship with your parent. The alternative is a lifetime of regret. You can decide later how you choose to interact with your surviving stepparent.

Integrity Versus Despair

In this phase of relationships, you come face to face with Erikson's integrity versus despair stage of life. Can you hold your head up high and be proud of your behavior toward Mom or Dad and your stepparent? Or do you hang your head in shame? Most likely your deceased parent would not want you to continue to carry some flag for them by excluding or disliking your stepparent. Life-altering events, such as death or divorce, stimulate reflection. You may ponder your behavior toward your stepparent or your support of Mom or Dad. If you have successfully resolved conflicts in the other stages of your relationships, chances are you will have a sense of fulfillment. More than likely you have endured all things while developing kindness, compassion, and other traits associated with charity. Though grieving, you may rejoice having maintained loving relationships. You can continue association with other family members without guilt or regret.

Contrast the rewards of loving ties with the consequences of broken bonds. Perhaps feelings of mistrust persisted throughout your parent's remarriage, or you resisted their efforts of kindness and alienated yourself instead. Resultant feelings of despair or disgust now afflict you. If you find yourself in this predicament, you aren't stuck. You can reverse your attitude and behavior as Max's stepsiblings did, thereby replacing despair with hope—hope of establishing loving relationships.

Take Action

Throughout your parent's remarriage you opposed it and refrained from participating in family activities. Now your stepparent has died. Stepsiblings rally around Mom or Dad. You stand on the sidelines, wanting to reach out but not knowing how. Here are possible actions you could take:

- Attend the funeral. Apologize to your parent for your lack of support and offer assistance.
- Thank stepsiblings for their support forMom or Dad and offer your condolences.
- Acknowledge your stepparent's passing by sending a condolence card to your parent.
- As time passes, help your parent solidify fond memories of the period of his or her life with your stepparent.

Possible Scenario
During your dad's marriage, you and your stepparent became good friends. Now that they've divorced, you want to maintain your friendship.

Child: I hope you know how much I love and appreciate you for all that you've done for my dad and our family during your marriage.

Stepparent: I feel your love and thank you for the friendship you've given to me.

Child: I would like to remain a part of your life and have your influence in the lives of my children.

Stepparent: I would like that too. Your children have stolen a piece of my heart.

The Heart of the Matter
Disaster, divorce, or death eventually strikes every marriage. Yet again, grieving confronts you, and you are left to pick up the pieces of your life and decide how to interact with the stepparent and stepsiblings who became part of your life. Whatever contact occurs with your stepparent, let your behavior be gracious and charitable. Remember that you didn't get the

divorce. Just because your parent divorces your stepparent does not mean you have divorced your stepparent. It's a choice.

- Following your parent's divorce, maintain whatever level of familiarity with a former stepparent that is comfortable and appropriate. Interactions may continue with a stepparent or stepsiblings with whom you have developed friendships. Contact may become uncomfortable if the stepparent remarries. Even a close friendship may become uncomfortable after a divorce. Be respectful and don't take it personally if contact is severed. If you disapproved of the marriage and are happy it is over, remember that you are an adult and act civilly and graciously in any chance meetings.

- Your relationship during the marriage usually determines the association you maintain after death. Other factors, including what is comfortable and appropriate, play a determining role in your subsequent interactions. Be considerate of your stepparent following the death of your parent. Afford them the respect befitting their position as your parent's spouse. Be charitable by maintaining contact and including them in family activities as desired and appropriate.

CHAPTER 11

"We're One Big, Happy Family!"

*"Stepfamilies experience most of their troubles
in the first two years."*

—*Virginia Rutter*

Congratulations! You've made it past the terrible twos. Some days you wondered if that stage would ever end. Think of how far you've come in that two years, or four, or seven, or however long it's been for you. You survived the wedding only to be confronted with figuring out your role as a stepchild. You weathered the holidays with changes to family traditions. Then you were hit with divided loyalties. That was a big mess until everyone learned to work as a team rather than interacting as competitors. Inheritance issues created a larger mess as emotions were jerked around along with the changes to wills and squabbles over family treasures. No wonder you are emotionally drained and feel like you've just stepped off a roller coaster. Despite challenges many marriages succeed, and everyone involved becomes one big, happy family.

In two short years, a toddler learns to crawl, walk, run, talk, and a host of other skills. In two long years, what have you learned? Perhaps you have come to realize that Mom or Dad and your stepparent truly love each other. They enjoy being together. They support and care for each other. They have a good marriage. They have tried to maintain and create a relationship with you. You've learned to trust all over again, to voice your opinions without forcing them on others, to initiate interaction and activities to get acquainted. You've learned your role in the new family configuration and mastered social skills to develop a genuine friendship with your stepparent. Each and every achievement is a step toward that "striking human achievement" in creating a nurturing life.

The realization of successful relationships includes at least one more lesson—the balm of forgiveness to heal emotional pain. If you have experienced a broken bone, a serious injury, or health condition requiring medical attention, you appreciate the body's ability to heal itself. The human body is amazing, often leaving no physical sign of injury. Some conditions require medical intervention for the healing process to begin. You are willing to pay whatever cost to reduce the pain and suffering. What a relief it is to be free of the physical pain! What about emotional pain? Can it be relieved? Yes, but the treatment requires effort on your part and may need professional intervention. Overlooking simple mistakes, apologizing for your errors, and forgiving others of theirs are prescriptive measures of compassion for healing emotional pain.

Compassion offers an emotional balm for ill feelings caused by offenses, aids in recognizing what is and is not acceptable behavior, teaches valuable lessons, and gives durability to relationships—building blocks of successful, happy stepfamilies. While compassion may be expensive in terms of pride, it yields great rewards of tenderness, mercy, and freedom from regret and guilt. In addition to improved emotional health, it also improves your physical and spiritual health. In the end you are grateful to have paid the price to relieve the pain and remove the guilt.

You have wonderful tools that help you practice compassion, including hearing, seeing, and your intuitive sense of feeling. These innate tools increase your sensitivity to the feelings and needs of your parent and stepparent. You listen to them for understanding. You notice unspoken feelings conveyed through their body language. Sometimes you sense deeper feelings that may be covered by surface words and mechanical actions.

The transition into a parent's remarriage can be a personally rewarding and growing time for you. Yes, it has its stresses as does every transition, but it can also be highly uplifting given some time. A variety of challenges tests a family's strength and durability. Throughout your parent's courtship and remarriage, more than likely you and your family experienced difficulties. Offenses occurred when mistakes were made—a missed birthday, a forgotten recital, a critical word. It is hard to be compassionate when you feel that you are the victim and have done nothing wrong or when you are hurting. These experiences provide opportunities for personal growth and the creation of harmony through compassion. Your willingness to overlook errors, to apologize for your mistakes, and to forgive brings desired healing to you and to your stepparent. Compassion bonds your family together, carries you through good times as well as bad, and builds loving friendships.

Experience—a Noble Teacher

"In every adversity there lies the seed of an equivalent advantage. In every defeat is a lesson showing you how to win the victory next time."
—*Robert Collier*

You have probably heard the television and radio emergency broadcast warning, "The following is a test. It is only a test," followed by sixty seconds of buzzing. This warning is relevant to stepfamilies. Life is a test filled with joyous and heartbreaking situations. Personal experiences, good and bad, affect emotions and are indelibly embedded in your memory. Experience is the teacher that creates opportunities to learn and to prepare for the test of nurturing relationships. The test is applying what you have learned to family interactions. You hope to learn your lesson well in order to replicate successes and to avoid repeating challenging situations. Sometimes you may feel like a failure because you repeat the same mistakes, but remember that you have many opportunities to learn until you get it right. Other times you learn quickly from your errors, modify your behavior or opinions, and continue to learn other valuable lessons. You may even do things right the first time with your stepparent and enjoy feelings of contentment and happiness. Each experience becomes a cherished teacher imparting priceless wisdom to enhance your personal growth and to bless others.

Spiritual writer Eileen Caddy said, "Dwell not on the past. Use it to illustrate a point, then leave it behind." This advice has significant application to mature stepfamilies. You cannot return a deceased parent to life or restore the marriage of divorced parents, but you can support your living parent and reach out to his or her spouse with love and acceptance. You can use your senses to hear the emotions behind the words, to notice the joy or pain, and to hear the plea for friendship. Act on feelings of compassion. Choose to affect the future by extending an outstretched hand today.

Marie's mother died when her children were young, and her father married a "vicious, old woman." Marie commented, "My stepmother was mean to my father and always criticized him. For Christmas she invited both sides of the family to visit at the same time. She didn't try to blend the families to make a new family. It was obvious that she favored her children and grandchildren. I vowed that if I were ever in a similar situation,

I would work hard to blend the two families to make a new family."

Marie experienced the heartache of unkind treatment toward her father and of favoritism toward her stepsiblings. Several years after her first marriage ended in divorce, Marie remarried. Rather than dwelling on the past and allowing her previous experience to embitter her, Marie was filled with understanding and love for her husband and his family and used the wisdom she gained to bless and enrich their lives. She worked hard to develop a relationship with her stepchildren, to welcome them into her life, and to help them feel comfortable in her home. She extended herself in every way to embrace them as her own children and treated her step-grandchildren as if they were her own grandchildren. Marie learned her lesson well. Instead of showing favoritism, Marie treated them equally with love. She honored her vow and developed enriching relationships by nurturing their lives.

Understanding is a key to acceptance. Katie's desire to understand her stepmother, Beverly, helped with her acceptance. "I think people are created from their experiences. When I look back at my childhood, I realize how fortunate I was. My parents wanted to be parents. We weren't a burden to them, and they wanted to spend time with us. Dad has always wanted to sit down with his children and take the time to teach us. I don't want to give up that relationship with my dad. I had that blessing, but my stepmother didn't. I try to understand her past to understand her needs now. Beverly had very difficult parents, so she's still like a child wanting to be assured she's okay." Katie recognized her relationship with her dad as one of her most priceless possessions. She learned that not everyone, including her stepmother, enjoyed the advantage of loving parents. Understanding and accepting her stepmother is Katie's way of preserving, protecting, and fortifying her relationship with her dad.

Love and acceptance are basic human needs. It takes a great deal of maturity to recognize these unmet needs in others and to offer unconditional love. Stepfamilies teach this lesson for those willing to learn. When the unconditional love is accepted and reciprocated, nurturing occurs.

Sandy also learned the power of unconditional love. "I feel unconditional, fatherly love from Dean. I could never say that Dean is my dad—that doesn't feel right—but in his actions he is my dad because he's proved to me that he loves me as much as my mom does. I've learned that someone can love me as much as my parent." Unconditional love and acceptance helped Sandy feel they have become one big, happy family.

The death of a parent poignantly teaches the value of association and contact. You never know when a loved one will die. Death cuts off all opportunities of association, and then it is too late to change that relationship. However, you can value your living parent and his or her spouse by spending time together to enhance those relationships, which increases your appreciation of your stepparent. Without association, the happy family rarely materializes.

Jeff's mother died before he married. "My mom and I were very close. I've learned that I didn't have enough time with her before her death. If I were in a situation similar to my dad's, I would make a greater effort to associate with my kids. I would keep in contact with them by spending time with them, calling them on the phone, and e-mailing them." Jeff admitted neither he nor his father is good at maintaining contact. His father has remarried three times. Jeff's wife and stepmothers usually initiated interaction.

Experience taught Sandy the importance of overcoming childish behaviors. It is easy to slip into a parent/child relationship and expect parents to do things for you and to care for you as they did when you were young. Sandy said, "I feel like I have grown up since my mom and Dean married. Mom's life is her life, and it doesn't need to revolve around me, which it had always done. We were everything to her and all of a sudden we weren't. I had to learn to grow up, which I never knew I had to learn. It was an experience of understanding people on a different level."

Parent/child relationships and interactions evolve as children mature. Acting and thinking as an adult enhances your ability to assess situations without jumping to conclusions. Ideas and opinions may differ, but lives are enriched as ideas are shared and respected.

From his experience Mike learned to accept reality and to share his feelings. Mike disagreed with some things his dad did during his courtship and remarriage, so he talked with his dad and shared his feelings with him. "My dad's remarriage has tested my responses to things that he does. I let him know I wasn't happy with how he handled situations and I thought his behavior was wrong. I've been more open with him about concerns. I tell my dad things that I shrugged off before my mom died. I have more of an open relationship with my dad, and it is easier to talk to him. I've learned that my dad is my dad no matter what decisions he makes in his life. There's nothing I can do about that. So I can choose to accept what he does or not. If I don't accept it, what good is it doing me?" Mike's willingness to share his feelings with his dad helped him to adjust to his dad's marriage, to strengthen their relationships, and to include his stepmother in their activities. They enjoy congenial associations.

Life's experiences are opportunities to learn compassion, which can be applied to developing harmonious families. Take time to reflect on your experiences. What have you done right? What mistakes have you made? What could you have done differently? The answer to each of these questions will give you valuable insights that you can apply toward improving your relationships. The time and effort you invest to learn from your experiences and to nurture your priceless family ties will pay you dividends in return.

Overlook Simple Mistakes

"Keeping score of old scores and scars, getting even and one-upping, always make you less than you are."
—Malcolm Forbes

Overlooking trivial errors provides another avenue of nurturing happy stepfamilies. Your parent's remarriage includes opportunities for you to overlook trivial mistakes in order to build lasting relationships. You are probably no stranger to being offended or inadvertently causing offense by something said or done. At times ignoring simple mistakes challenges your best intentions when you are hurting internally. The faster you overcome pride and overlook trivial errors, the happier you are as an individual and as a family.

Mistakes are part of life. You probably remember making silly errors on tests in school that significantly affected your score. Some teachers provided a retake of the exam for you to improve your grade. Thank goodness for those teachers. If only you had a retake test to undo simple mistakes in relationships that cause offense, life would be great. Though mistakes cannot be undone, they can be overlooked. Certainly, you appreciate family overlooking offenses you may cause. This step of compassion tempers judgment. You begin to discern between trivial incidents and significant ones.

Mike shared his reaction to potentially hurtful comments: "My dad's wife said some things that were sort of weird, out of place. You just smile and chuckle when that happens and go about your business." Mike remembers inappropriate comments being made, but he doesn't remember specifics, and that it is how it should be. They were trivial comments. A triviality is something that you probably will not remember in a year, so why stew over it now? No harm was intended, no offense was taken, and Mike and his stepmother maintained their relationship.

Referring to the incident on her dad's wedding day when her stepmother called her "daughter," Trudie reflected, "I realized that my dad's wife was in an awkward situation. Helen joined our family without knowing us personally. I know she meant 'daughter' as a term of endearment; however, the term was awkward for me. I tried to be gracious, but my body language betrayed me. I really didn't want to spoil Helen's wedding day. I had to overlook that as I have tried to establish a better relationship with her. That is in the past now, and things have improved."

The comments or behavior of others may adversely affect you, just as your comments or behavior may offend others. Things said or done with the best of intentions may produce a surprise response. These occasions test your ability to focus on the relationship by overlooking the ill-placed comment or behavior.

Kristen was surprised by her emotional reactions to certain events. For example, Kristen wondered what it meant about her family's position within the new marriage when her stepmother returned photos to her, especially when Kristen saw pictures of Mary's children in her dad and Mary's home. Kristen said, "Now Mary sees my kids as her grandchildren, but it has taken a little bit of time for that to happen." As Kristen stood back and thought about the incident, she realized that Mary meant no offense. Kristen overlooked Mary's gesture and allowed time for the relationship with her stepmother to evolve into a cherished, lasting friendship unencumbered by hurt feelings.

Had Kristen not exercised compassion by trying to understand and to overlook her stepmother's behavior, the outcome would have been quite the opposite. Recognizing that it takes time to develop enduring friendships, Kristen chose to use her energy to understand rather than being jealous or vindictive. She focused on the person rather than the act, thereby nurturing their relationship.

Life's experiences test your ability to exercise compassion by learning to govern your thoughts and guiding them to control your words and behaviors. When tempered by overlooking trivial errors, your experiences bond you with your parent and his or her spouse. It is often by mistakes that you grow and learn. At times your patience may be tested. Your ability to empathize increases by overlooking the simple mistakes of your stepparent. You continue to forge loving relationships.

Apologize Quickly

> *"Yes, there are times when something is legitimately not our fault. Blaming others, however, keeps us in a stuck state and is ultimately rough on our own self-esteem."*
> —Eric Allenbaugh

At times "I am sorry" are the three hardest words to say. You are admitting that you are not perfect. You made a mistake. Your error caused pain to others. It is difficult to admit you are the cause of the suffering. Perhaps if you say nothing, the pain will go away and everything will be forgotten. That usually does not happen. An apology is warranted for the healing to begin. A compassionate heart recognizes the ache you have caused, wants to relieve the pain, and inspires you to overcome pride by saying, "I'm sorry." Not only does your apology allow those offended to begin healing, but something about saying "I'm sorry" softens your heart as well.

Friction results when an apology is warranted but not extended. Abby related this experience: "More than a 'simple' mistake was made by a stepsister's spouse, which resulted in great inconvenience and monetary expense on our part. There has been no apology or restitution to us. We continue to attend their children's special events, but we don't get involved or interact with their family in any other way. So a slightly strained close relationship is now very strained."

When financial and emotional burdens of mistakes are not relieved, the sting remains and makes interactions uncomfortable. The whole family may feel the strain of the damaged relationship. A sincere apology offers an olive branch to the one offended, relieves the sting, and allows hearts to heal and relationships to mend. Reimbursements of monetary loss because of personal behavior or an effort to relieve emotional suffering through some type of restitution are additional corrective steps representing a desire to make the relationship the priority.

A **Parent's** Perspective

Meg offered the following advice: "Make sure that you don't make a joke out of something that is serious. It could really hurt someone's feelings. A couple of times, Ken made what he thought were comical statements to my children that caused misunderstanding. He had to apologize for his comments and state that he hadn't really meant what he said. You have to be careful when you speak and think about how your words will affect the people hearing them. If more people would develop the habit of thinking before acting, there would be much more serenity in relationships."

For eighteen years Debbie blamed her stepmother for the lack of relationship with her father. Debbie described her situation:

205

"I have never had a relationship with my dad. I am the only girl in my family, and I always felt rejected. I never felt good enough. I rebelled in every possible way. My relationship with my dad was just never the way I wanted it to be. Initially, I blamed it on my dad's job, his lack of affection, and problems with communication. Then I blamed my relationship with my dad, or lack thereof, on his wife. It was her fault, she did not want me around, and she never wanted kids. All these things I made up in my mind. In reality, my stepmother had never done or said anything that would make those things clear to me. I punished her by treating her badly, fighting with her, and talking about her to anyone who would listen. I really played the victim. My relationship with my dad suffered. I didn't try to mend things with him. I let our relationship go after my dad married."

Debbie shared the process she began eighteen years after her dad's marriage that led her to apologize to her stepmother, Jana: "The first step was attending a training conference in Las Vegas during which I came to a full realization of what I had done. I learned the 'facts' of what had happened versus what I had made up as the facts in my mind. The fact was that this woman married my dad. What I made up in my mind was the whole 'wicked stepmother' thing. After realizing what the situation was, I thought about it, talked it over with my 'life coach,' and came to understand that I really was the blame for all of the hurt I felt. After my 'breakthrough'—the realization of what the situation really was—it was four or five days before I apologized. I wanted to think about my realization and let it set in. I wanted to think of exactly what to say so I didn't sound like I was blaming my problem on my stepmother. I wanted Jana to know that I was taking full responsibility for our relationship. Jana tried to change the subject a few times, but she understood what I was saying, and she accepted the apology. We shared a hug, a real heartfelt hug. And we both cried. To feel the release of all that pent-up anger was amazing! I feel so free. I feel more positive about this relationship and the one with my dad. It is very liberating to discover the truth in yourself and to actually know it with surety, deep in your heart. I learned the importance of separating the facts from what you make up in your mind. Differentiating between reality and preconceptions is a very hard thing to do, but it is essential. Parents' separation is rarely easy for anyone—divorce happens. And when it does, we need to learn to live with it in a positive way."

Taking Hold of the Situation

Debbie's experience teaches valuable insights. First, desire a better relationship. As long as you play the victim, you will wallow in self-pity. Second, determine the facts and weigh them against "perceived reality." Perceptions are powerful and have a tendency to overshadow truth. Searching for truth leads you to dismiss false perceptions and to accept responsibility for your errors, this is the third insight. You begin to recognize the consequences of your behavior on others and yourself. You want to make amends. The fourth insight is the power of apology—saying "I'm sorry" releases pent-up emotions, liberates you from bonds of guilt, and heals your pain.

Not everyone thinks before speaking or acting, and when offense occurs it can cause an imbalance in the relationship. One individual views a remark or behavior as a simple mistake, while the other is deeply hurt. An apology is reasonable to expect. Saying "I'm sorry" helps erase errors and clear up misunderstandings. An apology removes the imbalance by leveling the error, replacing the strain in relationships with serenity.

An offense is much like a sliver; it gets under the skin, causes discomfort, and can lead to infection unless removed. When removed quickly, the pain ceases. Misspoken words get under the skin, cause heartache, and can lead to emotional disease unless corrected quickly. When offense occurs and is treated early, misunderstanding can easily be corrected before it festers, causing further injury and becoming more difficult to correct. Sometimes the offending individual is oblivious to the offense. If you have been hurt by your parent or stepparent and cannot get over it, accept the responsibility to let the offending party know what he or she did or said that was hurtful. Stepparents are not mind readers, but they are usually happy to make things right when they are aware of the problem, just as you would be.

Forgiveness Offers Healing

"To forgive is the highest, most beautiful form of love. In return, you will receive untold peace and happiness."
—Dr. Robert Muller

Whether mistakes are small or big, intentional or unintentional, forgiveness is the balm of relieving emotional pain. Forgiveness is easier and more beneficial when preceded by an apology. While some people struggle to say "I'm sorry," others don't feel an apology is necessary if they don't think they have done anything wrong. Yet others quickly apologize at the slightest intimation of offense. Regardless of the circumstances, forgiveness helps sooth the wounded heart.

Being offended by something said or done is a choice you make that injures your relationship and hinders healing. There are daily opportunities to seek and offer forgiveness in family relationships. We all can offend, often without intending to. Rather than dwelling on the mistake and allowing it to canker your soul, forgiveness permits you to put it behind you and move on. Stop telling stories about what offended you and realize how you feel is your choice.

Debbie's experience (in the previous subheading) is a prime example of playing the victim. Debbie was deeply hurt by the lack of relationship with her father. She found it easy to blame her stepmother for her problematic relationship. She created a grievance story and shared it with anyone who would listen. Debbie kept the hurt alive for eighteen years by retelling it.

When others have made mistakes and you have taken offense, these wrongs are stored in your memory bank. Withdrawals are made with each retelling to anyone who will listen. Reliving the experience makes you vulnerable to the accompanying emotions. Once forgiven you never need to make a withdrawal again. No one likes to be reminded of his or her errors. If the pain lingers, focus on the present and look forward to the future. Glean what knowledge and wisdom you can from your experiences, then don't look back at them. In this way you exercise compassion to affect your present and future relationship for good. Just as aerobic exercise strengthens your heart, compassionate exercise increases your heart's capacity for tenderness and mercy.

In a time when many are looking for a quick and easy way to solve relational problems, it is easy to overlook forgiveness. Yet the benefits of forgiveness not only mend relationships but also solve resultant problems in all aspects of life. Why not give forgiveness a try if you are burdened with emotional pain?

Debbie's experience portrays the healing benefits of forgiveness. Accepting the situation for what it really was rather than how she perceived it released Debbie as a victim. Accepting reality empowered her to make choices benefiting her father, stepmother, and herself. Debbie's apology and her stepmother's subsequent forgiveness freed Debbie from bonds of anger and bitterness and gave her hope for a better relationship with her loved ones. Freedom, affection, and happiness are some of the rewards of forgiveness.

Forgiveness means letting go of anger and hurt, thereby allowing peace to fill your heart. It means accepting a sincere apology and recognizing that slip-ups and mistakes occur that are unintentional and should be forgiven. Forgiveness allows relationships to flourish by bonding hearts together.

Lack of forgiveness allows the wrong to continue to occupy your thoughts. You may focus on your festering pain and wallow in self-pity. Relationships become stagnant or deteriorate. Years after the incident when her mother abandoned her bereaved brother after the death of his wife, Diane still feels the sting of rejection. Between a trip and a cruise, Diane's mother stopped to see her newest grandchild only to discover her daughter-in-law died after childbirth. Rather than staying to help her grieving son, Diane's mother returned to her home to go on the cruise with her new husband. Diane is working through feelings of rejection by maintaining contact with her mother and developing a relationship with her stepfather. Yet many choose misery by continuing in their self-pity. Why would anyone choose this option instead of choosing happiness through forgiveness?

Avoid Repeating Mistakes

"Insanity: doing the same thing over and over again and expecting different results."
—*Albert Einstein*

Once mistakes are forgiven, don't repeat them. Whether committing the error or being the victim of one, you are aware of the effects of those mistakes. Repeating errors adds insult to injury and impedes healing and progress. Misery accompanies stagnant or decaying relationships. Joy comes from growth and improvement in your life and relationships. If something you have said or done caused offense, it will probably inflict additional pain if repeated. It is best to try something different and hope for a better outcome.

Even if you don't understand why your mom or dad and stepparent were offended, you have to accept their feelings and take action. Their perception is what is true for them, and you cannot control that. Apologize, make reparations, and try not to repeat the offensive behavior.

Marie lives in the same town as her daughter, Janie, who visits frequently. Remember from a previous chapter that Marie's husband, John, and Janie had a blowup over her dog trampling through John's garden, a recurring behavior. The blowup brought the issue to light. There was a problem. They discussed it and reached a mutual agreement, eliminating the recurring problem and relieving tension. The incident was not repeated, and everyone was happier.

You may be oblivious to how your actions affect others. It takes another person to recognize the problem and love those involved enough to discuss the problem and focus on finding solutions. Mutual compassion aids in understanding the other's predicament and working together for a solution; implement the solution and avoid repeating the error.

Katie and her sisters learned quickly what things offended their dad's new wife. They discussed mistakes they made to avoid repeating them. Katie and her sisters also share things they have done that have improved their relationship with their stepmother and helped Beverly feel comfortable in their homes. Through their efforts and patience their relationship with their stepmother has improved. The emphasis Katie and her sisters placed on loving their stepmother forged a trusting relationship.

Wouldn't it be nice to have a retake for your behaviors? You could study your errors to improve your understanding of offenses, relive the situations and avoid problematic behavior, and thus improve the outcome. Relationships are not that easy, but whatever improvement you make is worth the effort. You have no rewind button to undo the past, but you have a mind to process errors and avoid making similar mistakes. Your experience develops compassion and prepares you to meet the challenge the next time it arises. Armed with understanding, your revised behavior produces a happier outcome, which makes happier lives and happier families.

Happiness Versus Misery

The terrible twos, whether it be childhood or the first two years of your parent's remarriage, eventually pass. Physical messes, such as a scraped knee or spilled milk, are much easier to resolve than the emotional turmoil of a family relationship. Yet these messes can be resolved by learning from your experiences as well as those of others. Learn what leads to happiness in family life and what destroys it. Overlook trivial errors. Apologize for mistakes quickly. And forgive rather than holding onto grudges. Embrace your mother or father and stepparent and say "I love you." You will be well on your way of achieving that "striking human achievement" of a nurturing family.

Take Action

Many suffer emotional pain, sometimes for years as Debbie did, due to unresolved grievances. Some heartache is self-inflicted from misperceptions, while other pain results from the ill behavior of others. Regardless of the cause, you want to know how to resolve the conflict to relieve your suffering. First, accept responsibility for your feelings. That does not mean you have to condone or like what happened to you. It means you are in control of you. You determine how you respond to your emotions. Next, change the present by making yourself the hero. You can't change the past. What's done is done. But you can alter the present. Debbie made herself the hero of her story by apologizing to her stepmother. You, too, can become the hero by offering a sincere apology. If you are not quite ready to apologize or to forgive, turn your thoughts away from the hurt. Stop relating your grievance story. Stop reliving it. A third option is to write down your story. Include your grievances and how they affect your life. Then write down what you would like to happen and the results you desire. Give your story a happily ever after ending.

Possible Scenario

For two years you've held a grudge against your dad and stepmother for giving you gift certificates for your birthday and Christmas. The tension you feel whenever you are together motivates you to discuss the issue with them.

Child: Something has been bothering me for a while, and I've decided to share it with you.

Parent: What's the problem, honey? We would never intentionally offend you.

Child: I know you wouldn't. That's why I decided to share it with you. Every time you give me a gift certificate and Jane's children gifts, I feel like you don't care enough about me to spend the time shopping for something I would like.

Stepparent: I am so sorry. The first Christmas we were married I didn't know what to give to you. You seemed so appreciative of the gift certificate we gave you. I thought you would prefer selecting something for yourself. Now that I know you prefer a gift, we can do that.

Child: Thank you. That would mean so much to me.

The Heart of the Matter

Throughout the test of life right and wrong choices are made that either cause offense or promote peace. Happy stepfamilies result from choices promoting peace. Unhappiness and sorrow result from poor choices. Study the outcome of family behavior to make more right choices and fewer errors and enjoy enhanced physical, emotional, and spiritual well-being. The choice is yours, but here are some behaviors that promote harmony by adding mercy and tenderness to your relationships:

- Experience is your best teacher in acquiring wisdom for making good choices. Learn from experience, yours and others, what promotes loving relationships then do it. Share your wisdom with other family members to avoid hurtful behaviors. Use your experience and common sense to discern what is significant and merits discussion and what is petty and should be ignored. Differentiate between important and trivial issues when challenges arise and deal with them appropriately. Make your family a priority by focusing on your relationships, rather than the trivialities, to develop compassion and to encourage happy families.

- Simple mistakes may cause you irritation; learn to overlook them. Move beyond the mistakes of the past and focus on the present. Be quick to overlook trivial comments or behaviors that you consider offensive or out of place, remembering that most offenses are unintentional. Take time to process the situation to gain understanding. Continue to offer compassion and friendship to your stepparent as your relationship evolves.

- Recognize when you have caused offense and be quick to apologize for misunderstandings or offensive behavior whether intentional or unintentional. If you are the one offended, tactfully share your feelings with your parent or stepparent to clear the air and restore serenity.

- Offer and accept forgiveness freely as a balm of emotional pain. Be sensitive to your stepparent's pain. If you have caused offense, ask for forgiveness. Rather than dwelling on offenses, be merciful and choose to forgive your parent or stepparent of their mistakes even if they don't apologize. Let go of anger and let the balm of forgiveness begin to soothe your pain and fill you with hope.
- Refrain from repeating behavior you know offends your stepparent. Observe what offends your stepparent, then don't do it. (That is stating the obvious, but sometimes it's beneficial to hear things stated bluntly.) Encourage discussion of problems and find acceptable solutions. Share insights with siblings of behaviors to avoid. Recognize what enhances family happiness, and then repeat those behaviors.

CHAPTER 12

"How Do I Overcome Barriers to Love?"

"Lots of people limit their possibilities by giving up easily. Never tell yourself this is too much for me. It's no use. I can't go on. If you do you're licked, and by your own thinking too. Keep believing and keep on keeping on."
—Norman Vincent Peale

H ave you ever considered your life and family relationships as works of art in progress? You are the artist of your life's masterpiece. You choose the design of your ultimate work of art—your relationships with others. What does your masterpiece look like now? What do you want it to look like when it's finished? Cultivating peaceful relationships with your parent and stepparent is an art. With love as the medium, you mix and blend courtesy, respect, kindness, and forgiveness, among other behaviors, to flow smoothly into your interactions, creating harmony. Just like with true works of art, at times with relationships it is best to stand back for a broader perspective of the whole picture, and other times you want to move in closer to examine the details.

You notice when Mom or Dad and your stepparent need time with all the extended family to work on unity, or time alone with you for the finer details of your relationship, or time for just the two of them. Like the artist, people make mistakes, and also like the master you've learned how to conceal them (overlook), blend them in (apologize), and to paint over them (forgive). Indeed, all aspects of a relationship—individuals, attitudes, behaviors, time, persistence, etc.—work together to produce the final outcome, your masterpiece.

Common Barriers

Barriers often crop up, preventing us from loving a stepparent and receiving love from him or her. Barriers impede the smooth flow of courtesy and respect, hampering your masterpiece of a loving relationship. Some of these barriers are rejection by your stepparent or by you, pessimism, mistreatment of your parent, and your parent's better treatment of a new spouse. Whether real or perceived, these barriers must be removed before your love can be the medium for free-flowing kindness. If you do the best you can to mix and blend good behaviors and the barriers remain, then you can still paint a work of art with your life. Regardless of what your parent and stepparent do, as long as you put forth your best effort to make the relationships work, you will be at peace—a masterpiece in and of itself.

You are not the only artist at work. For your relationships to truly become masterpieces, your mom or dad and stepparent must apply their own behaviors to the canvas. Your stepparent's attitude may be the barrier to giving and receiving love. His or her attitude and behavior affect your parent, which subsequently affects you. You can't change your stepparent's attitude, but you can control your own. Refuse to let it affect your attitude and continue kind deeds, thus applying good works to your relationship canvas. Respect your stepparent's right not to contribute to the masterpiece. There is comfort knowing you did all you could to nurture the relationship rather than being the barrier.

After Sarah's parents' divorce and her father's remarriage, Sarah felt like her dad turned his back on everything that was important to him and to her—her mom, his children, his church, his country—in order to appease his wife. Sarah and her sisters wondered about their father's love for them. They lived a long distance from their dad when he was ill and dying, so Sarah and her sisters were unable to care for him. Sarah related her final visit with her father: "My sisters and I decided to visit our dad before he died rather than attending the funeral. It was healing to all of us, and it meant the world to my dad. We never had the father/daughter relationship we all wanted, so we thought visiting him might be uncomfortable, but it wasn't. However, because my dad totally embraced his new wife and her family and excluded us, our visit felt superficial. My dad was a good man, he did his best, I knew he loved us, and he was dying. We all made our peace with that. My sisters and I felt like we had come full circle. We felt love and compassion for him and were grateful for the things he had provided for us."

Sarah's relationship was not what she desired. She lost the security of family and home when her parents divorced. Her father's remarriage and his wife's attitude heaped feelings of rejection on Sarah's already wounded heart. Yet she persisted in trying to include her dad and his wife in her life. Knowing she had done her best to have a loving relationship gave Sarah peace. Sarah's work of art (her relationship with her dad) changed several times throughout her father's life. She may have wondered if they were even working on the same painting, yet in the end they had their masterpiece —their mutual love.

Perhaps you experienced similar feelings when your parents divorced and later remarried. Watching your parent embrace a new spouse and stepfamily while ignoring you may feel like your love is being strangled. Your desire for your parent's love and acceptance is met with rejection. You may try to push your feelings of being rebuffed to the back of your mind only to have them resurface during a crisis. You discover your precious mutual feelings of love, still alive, struggle to be expressed.

Emotional Pain

Emotional pain is another barrier to giving or receiving love. Removing barriers prepares the canvas of your relationship for the painting to begin. It exposes your heart to love and be loved. Emotional pain is darkness inhibiting the artist from his work, inhibiting your natural desire to nurture your relationships. Freedom from emotional suffering is light that allows you to see clearly how and when to apply inclusion and thoughtfulness to your relationships. Nature symbolizes this phenomenon as some flowers, such as tulips, close to protect themselves when it is dark or cold. They open in full bloom when it is sunny and warm. Like the tulip, you may close up to protect yourself from cold and unkind behavior. However, you open up to receive the love and warmth of kindness and caring. The first intimation of caring opens your mind to the possibility of being loved by your parent and stepparent. Each additional act of kindness encourages you to give love in return. When their behavior is cold and uninviting, the best you can do is try to be warm toward them and hope their hearts will eventually open and reciprocate.

Some stepparents face the challenge of stepchildren not accepting them or the remarriage. Stepparents struggle with finding their place in their new family. Some adult children are reluctant to cooperate or be supportive, thus becoming the barrier to giving and receiving love. If you fall into this category, somehow you need to find a reason to reverse your negative feelings. Even a selfish reason such as your personal happiness is reason enough to make some effort to allow your relationship to be sketched on the canvas. Trudie said, "My stepmother feels like some of my siblings don't like her. She is probably right about some of them. She seems to be a people-oriented person, so it is hard for her not to be liked." Relationship masterpieces are halted before they even get started when adult children are unwilling to extend themselves.

Diane struggled with the loss of her mother's time, attention, and affection. When her mother abandoned her newly widowed son, Ted, and his four small children, Diane wondered if her mother would be available for her in a time of need. "I didn't understand my mother's behavior. I felt Mom was turning her back on Ted during a time of real need. Now I know that if something happens to my family, my mom may not be there. It hurts to think that I can't count on my mother because her husband needs her for a cruise or whatever," Diane said.

Pessimism and Negativity

Pessimism is another barrier that causes love to shrivel. Replace it with optimism to encourage love to blossom. Optimism increases through sincere efforts to serve and help each other in time of need. You notice a specific need of your parent or stepparent, and you give of your time to support her or him. You do so with the hope that your offering will be accepted and appreciated. Any display of concern and affection further increases your optimism and thereby nurtures your love. Find things to be positive about and use those thoughts to replace negative ones. As mentioned in previous chapters, Diane didn't give in to her feelings of pessimism. She nurtured her love for her mother by sending her mother phone cards, calling her frequently, and even calling Jim on Father's Day. Each act of service decreased Diane's pessimism and prepared her to open her heart to love her stepfather and to receive her mother's love. Your willingness to give of your time and abilities to serve your (step)parents will increase your optimism and strengthen your relationships.

Mistreatment

Mistreatment of your parent, whether real or perceived, is another barrier to love, which may afflict your relationships. Since the remarriage is your parent's decision, there is little you can do about mistreatment other than expressing your concern to your parent. If you are bold enough, you may even confront your stepparent. Continued efforts of kindness or service may encourage your stepparent to change his or her behavior, thus removing the barrier.

Diane feels that Jim takes advantage of her mother's gentle nature. "My stepfather is old-fashioned in that he sits on the couch and watches TV while my mom does everything for him. She rushes around making sure that he is settled. Part of me doesn't deal with that well. I think, 'Get off your hiney; she's retired too. You can get your own milk.'" Diane is concerned that her stepfather, who is still in good health, expects her mother to care for him even though she is aging.

On the opposite spectrum, like some children, you may observe Mom or Dad treating a new spouse better than she or he treated your other parent. In this case, your parent's behavior becomes the barrier for you to give love to or receive love from your stepparent. This barrier may create feelings of jealousy or disloyalty, with animosity directed to your stepparent.

Kristen worked through the challenge of seeing her dad treat his new wife differently and, in Kristen's mind, better than he treated her mother. Kristen explained how she overcame this barrier to love her stepmother: "One thing that was hard for me was I would see my dad immediately buy Mary things that my mother would ask for for years before my dad bought them for her. My dad and Mary go places together that dad would have balked about with my mother. There is a difference in the way that he treats Mary compared to how he treated my mother. Then I talked myself through it. Like, 'Kristen, just be real about it. At the beginning of a relationship you know people do whatever they do to make a good impression. When you've been married twenty years, fifty years, it doesn't work the same way as it does for newlyweds. You're not so concerned about impressing after years of marriage.' But that was hard for me seeing my dad buying Mary things."

Feelings of favoritism, as in Kristen's case, or of taking advantage of your parent, as in Diane's case, strain the joy that should be part of family life. Taking the time to understand the situation by studying it in your mind, like Kristen did, replaces negative feelings with a realistic comprehension of newlyweds. Your parent's marital relationship is a new love and is fragile, requiring additional attention. Newlyweds are on their best behavior to impress each other. This understanding may help you to view your stepparent and the marriage favorably. Another barrier to loving your stepparent begins to fall. You begin to notice and appreciate the improvements in a parent's life.

Overcoming Barriers with Personal Change and Positive Attitude

"No one is in control of your happiness but you, therefore, you have the power to change anything about yourself or your life that you want to change."
—*Barbara DeAngelis*

Circumstances are often the product of behavior. Since you are responsible for your behavior, you have the power to change your situation. If you are not content with your current relationship, accept responsibility and change yourself. Change is a precursor of progress. Wishing that others were different is counterproductive to growth and peace because responsibility for problems is placed on the other individual. No improvement will be made until you recognize your responsibility for some of the discontent. Wishing for a better relationship with your parent and stepparent becomes a powerful motivator to change when you remove the blinders and accept responsibility.

Since you can't change your parent and stepparent, your only alternative to improvement is to change yourself. Accepting the status quo seems a whole lot easier than making personal changes to alter your circumstances. You may even rebel against change, wondering why you are the one who has to change. Speaking frankly, you are the only one who can remedy your situation. Begin by formulating a picture of your desired relationship, and hold fast to your dream until the changes are set in motion and eventually become the norm.

Diane said, "I know that I need to try harder to have a better relationship with my stepfather. Parts of me want to try harder and parts of me just want to say 'whatever.' I have learned Jim's priorities. If something inconveniences him, then he's upset about it. But if it fits into Jim's plan, it's okay. The rebellious part of me doesn't want to cater to him, then the other part of me says that I need to make more of an effort for my mom's sake."

Diane's ambivalent feelings are the first intimation that change is necessary. Diane is unhappy with the current relationship and desires to improve it. She mentally debates her opposing feelings to change and why she has to be the one to change. Diane knows that all will benefit in the end, yet the decision is still a difficult one. Perhaps you have experienced a similar ambivalence. Once you determine the type of relationship you desire and seek to develop it, day-to-day decisions are made more easily without mental debate.

Katie experienced a few challenges with her stepmother on her way to developing a harmonious relationship. She recognized she could only change herself. Katie learned what annoys her stepmother and altered her behavior to achieve the peace she desires. Katie explained, "When Beverly voices an opinion, I accept that is her opinion. I don't try to sway her to mine. I've learned that's a hot button with her. I believe that we make our choices and we can change things. When Beverly describes a situation, it's always what other people have done to her. It's never her responsibility, but rather it's always somebody else's fault. My belief is that the only person I can change is me. I try to work from that, and in our relationship I change me not her." In the process Beverly also changed.

Changing yourself includes changing your attitude. Earl Nightingale said, "A great attitude does much more than turn on the lights in our worlds; it seems to magically connect us to all sorts of serendipitous opportunities that were somehow absent before we changed." Altering your attitude is probably the easiest way to overcome barriers to loving and accepting your stepparent. Attitude is the raw material that affects everything you do and say. If you are unhappy with your current situation, the simplest way to change it is to change your attitude. A poor attitude blinds us to kindnesses extended to us and to opportunities to be kind. Focusing on personal grievances makes us oblivious to the needs of others. On the other hand, a positive attitude reveals others' needs and magically alters your behavior to coincide with your desires. Therefore, your relationship (good or bad) with your parent and stepparent is dependent upon your attitude. Changing your attitude takes practice and effort. Eventually, you become skilled at improving your disposition and your relationships.

Sarah's mother has an attitude of acceptance. She has "magically" connected with her stepchildren and grandchildren. "My mom has spent time with her husband's children and with his grandchildren. John's first wife died of cancer, and my mom never tried to take her place. She knows she can't. John's two children live in a different province. They visit fairly regularly and they adore my mom. It would be hard not to. She just reaches out. It would be so hard as an adult woman not to have a mom, and I have a wonderful one. I am so proud of her for reaching out to her stepdaughter who no longer has a mother. I am so glad that she can have that kind of relationship with her stepdaughter," Sarah said.

Sarah's example of her mother, Marie, portrays the type of relationship possible when individuals have a positive attitude and reach out to embrace each other with love and kindness. Marie wants her stepchildren to know that she loves them, wants to be part of their lives, and wants them to feel welcome and comfortable in her home. Marie's wise and simple common sense mentality brought harmony into their relationship. Her behavior reflected her attitude. Sarah seems to have inherited a similar attitude. Rather than being jealous of her mother's attention to others, Sarah rejoiced that John's children benefit from her mother's affection.

Steve's positive attitude about his mother's marriage set the tone for developing a friendship with his stepfather. Steve was happy to learn that his mother was going to remarry. "Mom was lonely and it would be good for her to have another companion," said Steve. With that attitude, Steve extended a hand of friendship and developed a warm relationship with his stepfather. Steve's words and actions naturally expressed his approval. "I have tried to be friendly toward Nolan, greet him, shake his hand, visit with him when he's around, and just nurture the relationship as you would a friendship. I took the attitude from the beginning that this is a good thing because my mother was going to be happier and not lonely. That initial attitude helped. I wasn't second-guessing how things were going when there were ups and downs. Mom and Nolan's marriage has been good for me, my mom, and for my whole family."

A positive attitude about your parent's spouse and marriage frees you from possible false notions and allows you to nurture the relationship to develop unity. A negative or a wait-and-see attitude of the marriage and spouse prevents you from creating bonds and makes it harder to embrace your stepparent, possibly resulting in unkind behavior and leading to discord and unhappiness. Choose happiness by choosing a positive attitude.

Overcoming Barriers with Reasonable Expectations

"Expectations improperly indulged, must end in disappointment. If it be asked, what is the improper expectation which it is dangerous to indulge, experience will quickly answer, that it is such expectation as is dictated not by reason, but by desire; expectation raised, not by the common occurrences of life, but by the wants of the expectant; an expectation that requires the common course of things to be changed, and the general rules of action to be broken."
—*Samuel Johnson*

Like other children, you may have expectations of always having Mom or Dad available to help or visit you as needed. You may expect Dad to treat his wife in a manner similar to how he treated your mother. Or you may expect gender equality in Mom's marriage. Your parents may have promised you the family heirloom clock or other item that you have always wanted. These expectations seem reasonable until your parent remarries. Reality quickly hits and you realize that life offers no guarantees. You may have thought that this stepfamily business was already a challenge to make work. Unless you already decided to make your relationships the priority, you are confronted with the dilemma of coping with dashed expectations.

As a child you required a lot of time and attention. As you grew older, you became independent, responsible for yourself. If Mom and Dad gave you a lot of attention throughout your life, it can be emotionally difficult when that attention diminishes or is absent when your parent remarries. It is unreasonable for your parent to expect you to be jubilant about his or her marriage and welcoming of your new stepparent when you are feeling rejected or abandoned. Expecting your parent to give you as much attention after remarrying as he or she did prior to the marriage is also unreasonable.

Diane's mother devoted her life to raising and caring for her children and remained an active part of their lives when they married and had families of their own. That time and attention diminished after her mother remarried. Diane struggled with the loss of attention. Diane learned to accept the situation the way it is and to appreciate the efforts that her mother and step-father make to maintain a relationship with her. Diane said, "I have arrived at the emotional place that this is how much my mother is willing and able to give to me. I can't change it, so I just have to accept it and be happy with what she can give me. Sitting around wishing that Mom could do more or be more does not change the situation."

Subconsciously Diane expected her mother's attentive behavior to continue after her mom remarried. Then reality hit. Diane's idealistic expectation prevented her from enjoying fulfilling relationships with her mom and new stepdad. Dashed expectations are sometimes hard to cope with. Knowing that changes will occur when your parent remarries does not adequately prepare you for reality.

Eventually Diane realized and accepted that her mother's new husband, Jim, placed more demands upon her mother's time and attention, and Jim had children and grandchildren who received some of her mom's attention. Diane saw the evolution in the relationships. Noticing the happiness and new interests Jim brought into her mother's life helped Diane to accept Jim and to appreciate the time her mother spends with her. Diane had to adjust her expectations to make them reasonable and in line with reality. In the process she experienced greater peace.

Impractical Expectations of Personal Property

Unrealistic expectations are also made regarding personal property. You may expect to inherit specific items that your parents may have promised you. Some may even take it upon themselves to help themselves while parents are away. Brenda shared this example: "Patsy married Alex later in life, and both were widows. The couple returned to Alex's house from their honeymoon only to find that all the china in their china cabinet was gone. They almost called the police, but then discovered that their daughter-in-law, married to Alex's son, decided on her own to take what she wanted rather than let Patsy use it. Alex considered the china his, as well as his deceased wife's, and was rightfully upset because he had not given his daughter-in-law permission to have the china. Patsy was upset because she would never have prevented the family from having the china. Both were upset at the violation of trust—the key entrusted to Alex's son was used to virtually steal the dishes."

Unreasonable expectations assumed by or placed on you or your stepparent inevitably cause problems that affect relationships. Realistic expectations of time, attention, or inheritance overcome barriers of trusted relationships.

Overcoming Barriers Through Wise Choices

"If you approach life with a sense of possibility and the expectation of positive results, you're more likely to have a life in which possibilities are realized and results are positive."
—Lisa Funderburg

Wise choices often overcome barriers to friendship. Opportunities abound for those who travel through life with their senses alert for ways to help and serve others. You see, hear, or feel how you can be a source of strength, support, comfort, or encouragement to your parent and stepparent. Acting upon these opportunities to aid demonstrates your desire to be of service and lends itself to increased harmony within your stepfamily.

Steve's family experienced unity by reaching out to his stepfather. Giving Nolan a Christmas gift before he married Steve's mother was simple common sense and the right thing to do. Nolan would soon be part of the family, and Steve wanted him to feel included and accepted by the family. Nolan felt welcomed and reciprocated with gifts to Steve's family.

In order to maintain harmonious relationships, Katie and her sisters discuss how they can remain close to their father without offending their stepmother, Beverly. They looked for ways to build unity and acceptance into their relationships. At the same time they avoided doing things they knew cause discord. Maintaining a healthy relationship with their father and Beverly encouraged them to act wisely. Over time their stepmother relented to their requests of soliciting their father's time and advice.

As soon as Diane heard that her sister-in-law died, she flew to her brother's home to support and comfort Ted and his children. To Diane, family is a priority and helping her brother was the right and reasonable thing to do. Her mother and Jim's different priorities hurt Diane. She struggled with accepting Jim. Diane eventually sent Jim a Father's Day card from her children and was by his side when he was hospitalized. Diane did these things because they were the right things to do. Doing what was right softened Diane's heart. She received peace and a clearer understanding of her mother and Jim. Through her actions, Diane showed that when you love someone, you do what is reasonable and logical to support them through every circumstance.

A **Parent's** Perspective

Neal and Anne experienced increased harmony as they continued to nurture their relationship with Neal's children. Neal and Anne invite all of their children to family activities. Neal seeks opportunities to spend time with his children individually. They want their children to feel their love, so they seek to do what is right for the individual as well as the family.

Hurt feelings, disappointment, or other excuses may prevent you from doing what you know is right. Inaction delays healing and may cause discord. Sometimes when you are hurting, doing the right thing is difficult. However, choosing to do what you know is right begins the healing process, softens your heart toward the perpetrator of your disappointment, and may soften their heart toward you.

Learn to Laugh

Perhaps you've been in a situation with Mom or Dad and your stepparent where tension was so thick that you felt like you could cut it with a knife. Then someone made a humorous comment and the tension dissipated. Research studies now confirm laughter's benefits. In a Reader's Digest humor special, Dr. Dan Ferber discusses benefits of humor:

"A growing body of research suggests that humor can tune our minds, help us learn, and keep us mentally loose, limber and creative. . . . Amusement and other positive feelings make people think more flexibly and try more novel alternatives when solving a problem. All this suggests that by enjoying humor, playing and exploring, we can better understand ourselves, others and the world we live in. What's more, those changes last, and help us during hard times."

You may not need research to confirm what you've experienced firsthand, but you may need a reminder to use humor to relieve tension that creeps into your relationships.

In an essay entitled "Laugh in the face of adversity: I'm not kidding," Dr. Barry Bittman outlines four key elements of using humor as a coping mechanism.

Adaptation

The first key is adaptation. "In the context of 'adaptation,' the only things in life that are certain are death, taxes and change. The latter seems to cause the most stress for us. Anything that veers us away from a set routine causes some degree of distress. It's not surprising that people who adapt are also the ones who succeed. In the face of change, one can panic, become depressed and give in. Yet there's also the choice to laugh, take a deep breath, dig in and discover the best means to deal with new and challenging circumstances. Laughter in the midst of change can be a very effective 'time-out.' It signifies our resolve to view the issue or challenge in a more rational perspective. Humor provides the unique opening to move forward on a positive note."

Your parent's remarriage definitely falls into the category of change and presents challenges and opportunities to adapt. The first meeting, the wedding day, and visits home may present uncomfortable moments. Appropriate humor has the potential of putting people at ease. As mentioned previously, the first time Scott met his stepmother, Mary, he embraced her and greeted her with a unique, humorous opening line: "Am I going to have a sibling?" Mary laughed and immediately felt accepted and at ease. Scott's initial greeting helped both of them to relax and adapt to a new person in their lives. Their relationship started on a positive note and continued from there.

Stress

Dr. Bittner's second key element of humor is stress. Laughter helps to interrupt the harmful physiological consequences of stress. Feelings of insecurity from changes in your family after your parent's remarriage often increase stress levels. Mature stepfamilies can be a breeding ground for ill-placed remarks and unkind behavior. Resulting problems, if left unchecked, increase tension and may escalate to bigger challenges. Humor, used as a coping rather than a put-down mechanism, stems bitterness that may crop up. Changing your mindset from taking things personally to finding humor in the situation often saves the day by relieving tension. You choose to feel love and joy rather than sadness and animosity. Your ability to find humor helps you to remain calm when delicate issues arise that require increased sensitivity. An appropriate touch of humor brings laughter, releasing the mounting tension.

Marie uses humor to relieve tension by making an uncomfortable situation comfortable. "It's especially important to use humor when you are married to someone who is very strict and opinionated. Sometimes there is just no way but his way, so I'll make a big joke of the issue and tension dissipates from the whole situation." If you, like Marie, deal with stepfamily members who are opinionated, humor may save your day.

Choice

Dr. Bittner's third element of humor is choice. "Speaking of 'balance,' life is full of choices that serve to constantly tweak the quality and balance of our lives on many levels. The key word here is 'choice.' In the face of adversity, you can pack your bags and walk away sulking that life has just thrown you a curve. Yet if you choose to meet the challenge head on, laughter can pave the way past obstacles while progressively building a refreshing perspective for persevering against the odds. The bottom line is that we all have the choice to laugh, regardless of our circumstances."

Some late-life marriages end in divorce. The odds are stacked against them from the beginning if their children oppose their marriage and try to sabotage it. Some couples persevere, beating the odds. If your parent has a good marriage and is happy, help them beat the odds by choosing humor.

Rather than being offended by simple errors or unkind behavior, looking for the lighter side and choosing to laugh minimizes obstacles, making them easier to surmount. Melanie's dad and stepfather, Dan, have the same birthday and share similar physical characteristics. "For a long time my mom called Dan by my dad's name. Mom laughed about her error. Dan laughed about it. He has a great sense of humor. They both do," Melanie said. Dan looked for the lighter side and chose to laugh rather than be offended. No one was uncomfortable when the slip-up occurred.

A similar blunder happened to Mary, as mentioned in a previous chapter. Mary also laughed when the best man referred to her by the previous wife's name. Rather than being offended, Mary chose happiness and basked in the joy of her wedding day and the company of those she loved. Blunders like that happen. Why choose to be hurt when you can choose joy?

Everyone appreciates a good sense of humor. Families who learn to laugh together enjoy being together. They reminisce, retelling stories that occurred years ago. They see the humor not noticeable when the event happened. Why not see the humor now rather than waiting years to laugh, and avoid unnecessary stress?

Richard appreciates his dad's sense of humor. He couldn't think of a specific example but he remembers the effects of his dad's humor to relieve tension: "My dad has a sense of humor that he uses to lighten things up." His dad uses humor to tip the scale from tension to lightheartedness and normalcy.

Control

Dr. Bittner's fourth element of humor is control. Finding something you have control over reduces frustration and increases resiliency.

Although Dr. Bittner's advice is directed to patients with serious and life-threatening health problems, it is sage counsel for any situation where you feel out of control including awkward moments with your stepparent. Some stepfamilies experience adversity that may get out of hand if not controlled. When you feel out of control, you and your family suffer. Unity and harmony of family life are threatened. Humor gives you control by restoring some balance to your emotions. With reduced stress levels, you are calmer, and as a result, you use better judgment in your social decisions.

Dave and Ruth's sense of humor was evident during my interview with them. Ruth spoke of her daughter with mental disabilities: "All of my children focused on Janice. So they haven't had time to focus on themselves. We don't have any sibling rivalry, which I think is because of Janice."

"Gee, I thought it was because of me. After all of these years...," Dave teased.

"Oh dear, dear, I shouldn't have said that," Ruth quipped.

Both laughed. Their joy in being together was manifested through their humor. In their advanced years they appeared calm and in control of their situation, which was certainly aided by their willingness to laugh and choose humor. Ruth's children enjoy spending time with them, further increasing their joy as a family. Ruth added, "You have to have a sense of humor. You can't take life too seriously. We have a laughing good time when we get together."

Even though humor does not eliminate family challenges, it lessens the burden of tensions, allowing you to maintain control of your emotions and make sensible choices. Life is too short and ceases to be fun when you take everything personally and seriously. Some matters are serious and should be taken seriously. But almost every awkward situation viewed with a different light may be humorous. Indulge in laughter as one of life's simple pleasures to lighten your burdens and enjoy your relationships.

Humor has made it easy for Sandy to be with her mom and stepfather. "Dean loves jokes and he'll get the paper and read articles that are humorous, and laugh and laugh. He is so funny tears come to my eyes. The story isn't all that funny, but to watch him laugh is amusing. My mom's the same way. She gets the biggest thrill out of the silliest things, like funny jokes. Mom and Dean laugh a lot. When I'm with them, I laugh because they're jovial and have fun together. When I'm there, it's hard to be serious unless we're having a serious conversation because we're usually laughing," Sandy said. Obviously, Sandy enjoys the time she spends with her mom and stepdad. They have adapted well to each other and changes in their family by choosing laughter to maintain balance and control.

Humor helps families feel comfortable being together and relaxing together. Sometimes laughter brings tears to your eyes; it can also miraculously turn tears of sadness into joy. In the face of adversity, temper is your worst enemy while humor is your best friend. Humor puts you in control of your emotions and allows you to choose how you react to challenges.

Persistence Pays Dividends

"Don't be afraid if things seem difficult in the beginning. That's only the initial impression. The important thing is not to retreat; you have to master yourself."

—*Olga Korbut*

Failures and rejections occur periodically in stepfamily relationships, yet life can still be good, wisdom can be gained, and happiness experienced. Personal shortcomings or trials are part of life. Others can relate to you because they have their own shortcomings and troubles. In spite of challenges, many stepfamilies have developed close ties because of one individual's persistence.

A **Stepparent's** Perspective

Neal and Anne make continuous efforts to strengthen their family, not giving up on Neal's son and a daughter who are less accepting of their marriage. Neal talks to them and visits them. At times his son acts more comfortable when he is with the family than when they first married. Other times they wonder if they are making progress; nevertheless, they continue trying.

You were probably taught to get back on your bike when you fell off and try again and again until you succeeded. Falling down is not a failure. Failure occurs when you stop trying. Thomas Edison said of his attempts to invent the incandescent light bulb, "Our greatest weakness lies in giving up. The most certain way to succeed is always to try just one more time. If I find 10,000 ways something won't work, I haven't failed. I am not discouraged, because every wrong attempt discarded is often a step forward." You also need to pick yourself up after failure or rejection in relationships and try again. Be willing to finish your masterpiece. Trust, respect, and love may not come after the first, second, or third try. Sometimes it takes years of trying and persistent effort, but the change of heart that eventually comes is well worth the effort. Remember, your masterpiece is not finished until the final brush strokes are added. Celebrate the effort, not the result.

For seven years Trudie let her feelings of rejection hinder her relationships with her dad and his wife, Helen, before she planned another family activity. "It was fun getting together, playing, and talking. We have had several activities since then. I could tell that my children felt like strangers with their cousins. It's sad that I let my children grow up without knowing their cousins because of my hurt feelings. I learned the importance of trying again and again to develop family relationships," she said.

Because people persisted and tried again and again in spite of failures, modern transportation and technology allow you to easily contact and visit family members. Rather than becoming discouraged from failure, inventors learned what didn't work then continued to try something different. Their determination to pursue their dreams has made everything faster, easier, and more accessible for you. The same principle holds true for your stepfamily relationships. As you persist in your efforts to get along, to associate together, and to help each other, you increase feelings of acceptance, security, and harmony.

Time Is a Healer and Revealer

"Make each day useful and cheerful and prove that you know the worth of time by employing it well. Then youth will be happy, old age without regret and life a beautiful success."
—*Louisa May Alcott*

You've likely heard the expression "time heals all wounds." Physical injuries heal with time, sometimes without even a scar. But what about emotional wounds? Those acquainted with traumatic experiences know emotional pain does indeed lessen with time, but often it never heals completely. Time is also a revealer. Reflection on past experiences and challenges reveals insights that give you a fresh perspective on disquieting circumstances with remarriage. You may recognize personal mistakes and what you can do to improve your situation and your relationships. A different perspective opens your eyes to acceptance of your stepparent. You see what you can do to increase your parent's joy. Your *aha* insight begins to change your heart.

As you discuss past grievances or misperceptions with Mom or Dad and your stepparent, grievances are forgiven and misperceptions are clarified and replaced with comprehension. Time becomes a healer and a revealer.

Diane experienced heartache when she felt that her mother abandoned her brother in his time of need by going on a cruise with her new husband. Diane's heart turned away from her stepfather, Jim, because she felt he was the cause of the abandonment and, therefore, her heartache. Years after her mother's remarriage, Diane's heart softened toward her mother and Jim, and she desired to improve her relationship with both of them.

During a visit with Diane's family, Jim was hospitalized with acute pneumonia. "While Jim was in intensive care, my mom wanted to go clothes shopping. She shopped and shopped at the mall without a care. I said, 'Should we get back to the hospital?'

'Nah. There's nothing we can do really. All those people are taking care of him.'

'Are you worried about him?'

'No.'

'Do you think he's going to be mad at you?'

239

'What's he going to do about it?'

'Nothing I guess. Okay, if you're happy, I'm happy.' We shopped and shopped. We were gone several hours while Jim received medical care at the hospital. That conversation with my mom gave me a view of how my mom felt; she was obviously struggling too. It gave me the desire to try harder to make our relationships better. A big part of their relationship was Mom's pride. She was going to make the relationship work," Diane said. Time became a revealer to Diane. Ginny's attitude about her marriage revealed itself to Diane with added comprehension. Diane saw the effects of her behavior on her mother and wanted to change in order to improve their situation, thereby initiating the healing process.

Pain often blinds you to the situation of your parent and stepparent as it did Diane. You cope with an aching heart the best you can oblivious of how your behavior affects those you love. Although Diane was a victim of her mother's decisions, unwittingly Diane made her mother a victim of her behavior. Diane's disinterest in her stepfather affected Diane's mother and consequently their relationship. Diane's eye-opening experience revealed to her the effects of her attitude and behavior on her mother. Wow! She was part of the problem. Diane's new perspective of the situation gave her the desire to minimize her mother's burden by improving her relationship with Jim, thus becoming part of the solution.

If you feel like you are a victim of your parent's decisions, you may inadvertently let your emotions control your behavior. You want to act differently, but your heartache is overwhelming. Mom or Dad and your stepparent unintentionally become victims of your behavior while experiencing their own grief. *Aha* moments such as Diane's may give you a wake-up call, reveal insights, and precipitate change in you.

To overcome blindness of others' pain, set aside your suffering and try to put yourself in their shoes. This unselfish act enables you to be objective and comprehend their emotions and behavior. You realize that they, too, have hidden or buried sorrow. This new perspective tugs at your heartstrings, and you want to reach out to them with love and compassion. You desire to relieve the burden they carry because of your behavior. Time reveals your true intentions.

Interviewing adult stepchildren and mature couples softened and changed my heart. I experienced anguish and resulting physical pain from some of the things my dad did and said during his courtship and first year of his marriage to his new wife. I wanted to protect myself from further pain. I wore protective armor and became aloof in my interactions with my dad. My behavior affected my dad, and it hurt me too. I allowed my pain to blur my vision, affect my judgment, and stifle my ability to experience joy and happiness. Listening to the stories of others, gleaning their wisdom, and changing my attitude and behavior replaced my bitterness and anger with compassion and forgiveness. I understand my dad's behavior is typical for men. I accept and love my dad's wife, not as a mother and not to replace my mother, but as my dad's companion. I recognize comments I found offensive were not meant to be mean-spirited in any way. I see more clearly the happiness my stepmother brings to my dad and the support she gives to him. Time revealed my dad's intentions and my deepest desires.

Emotional pain may overwhelm you, causing you to withdraw and to quit trying to build relationships with your parent and stepparent. Quitting implies defeat. Never quit trying in your relationships. They are priceless and worth every effort you make to nurture them. Overcome the defeatist attitude by choosing one behavior to improve your relationships, for instance acceptance. Practice that before moving on to the next behavior, perhaps kindness and extending a hand of friendship. Follow that up with recognizing special events. Possibilities are endless for building loving, harmonious relationships. In the beginning phase of changing your heart, you may wonder if the inconvenience is worth the effort. Progress appears slow from day to day; however, over the period of a week or month the progress is more apparent. It may even take years. Focus on your dream of loving relationships and endure patiently the process of change. Let time reveal personalities.

At the beginning of a parent's marriage, it is common to suspect motives. You may adopt a wait-and-see attitude or a "guilty until proven innocent" attitude. Then you have your eye-opening experience and you recognize your stepparent is a good person. Sandy described her change of heart: "The way I felt at the beginning of Mom and Dean's marriage compared to the way I feel for Dean now is completely different. My heart has totally changed. I realize what a good man Dean is as I watch him take such good care of my mom. If my mother were alone, I would be more worried about her. I would feel like I needed to be more involved in her care. I don't have to worry about that because Dean is right there. Dean's companionship lifts a burden off my shoulders because I know that Mom is cared for. Now I can't even imagine why I had childish and selfish feelings at the beginning of their marriage."

As time reveals personalities, it allows you to judge fairly. Such was the case with Kristen when her father remarried. "I waited to see where the marriage was going. I suspended judgment. It has been a process for me. This new person came into my life. I'm thinking *What do I do with her? How do I feel about her?* Rather than saying, 'I don't like this.' I thought, *Okay, how is this marriage going to be?* I suspended judgment. I do judge now, but my judgments aren't harsh; rather, they are along the lines of 'this marriage is fine, this is great, this is wonderful.'"

Over time you forge your relationship with your stepparent. You receive bursts of insight that reveal changes you need to make, like accepting your stepparent, and working to lessen any burden your parent might carry. You desire to be better. You may balk about the changes you need to make, but once made, you wonder why you fretted over them. The changes make your relationships more enjoyable and comfortable. You are the recipient of your stepparent's love and friendship. When finished, you realize the change was not as hard as you thought it might be. Time reveals a beautiful masterpiece in progress.

The Heart of the Matter

Many people experience one type of barrier or another in their pursuit of healthy, happy relationships. Love is a key motivator of discovering a way to surmount each barrier.

- Barriers restrict your ability to give and receive love with your parent and stepparent. Correctly diagnosing the barrier is the first step toward removing it. Whatever the barrier, consider whether it is best dealt with individually or as a family. Persistent efforts to show love and support to Mom or Dad and your stepparent through kindness, service, or time to help remove the barriers, thus encouraging the giving and receiving of love.

- Accepting responsibility for your circumstances is the first step in overcoming the barrier of stagnation. If you are unhappy with your current relationships, assess the situation and determine what you can do differently to modify it. Knowing the type of relationship you desire is the second step. Visualize what you want and ascertain the changes you need to make. Implement the changes, and act in a manner befitting that relationship. The power lies within you to make your desired stepfamily life a reality. Progress may seem slow because it is a day-to-day gradual process. Little by little others recognize your efforts to ameliorate the situation, and eventually you notice that altered behavior in your stepparent. Personal change and a positive attitude overcome the barrier of a negative attitude. Attitude, yours and your stepparent's, affects behavior and ultimately your relationship. A positive attitude consistently portrayed in words and actions helps win the heart of a stepparent, if not at first, then usually in time. Through your behavior let your stepparent know of and feel your love and acceptance. Treat your stepparent as you would a friend.

- False expectations are another barrier to successful relationships. Reasonable expectations avoid disappointment, circumventing the barrier. Review and revise your expectations of yourself, your parent, and stepparent to make them reasonable.

- Poor choices also hamper friendship development. Consider the consequences of choices available to you. Ponder your needs and desires as well as those of your parent and stepparent. Implement ideas that come to you that will strengthen your relationships.

- Make wise choices to further harmonize your relationships by blessing your lives.

- Rewire your thoughts for humor to aid your adjustment to stepfamily relationships and to relieve stress. Cultivate humor by learning to laugh at mistakes. Rather than being offended, find humor in tense situations. Smile to put yourself and your stepparent at ease. Add humor to your interactions to better understand yourself, others, and your relationships.

- Successful relationships are the result of persistent effort. Continue to pursue healthy interactions and happy relationships even after rejection or failure. Persist in communicating love. Rewards of improved relationships are eventually reaped. If your goal of friendship is not achieved, persistence can be its own reward.

- Allow time to reveal your parent's struggles, your stepparent's personality, and your intentions. Permit time to heal heartache or disappointment.

Take Action

*"The perfect no-stress environment is the grave. When we
change our perception we gain control. The stress becomes a
challenge, not a threat. When we commit to action, to actually
doing something rather than feeling trapped by events,
the stress in our life becomes manageable."*
—*Greg Anderson*

You may have thought it would be nice to have a
training manual on your new stepparent or the new
personality inhabiting Mom or Dad's body since he or
she remarried. The manual might include likes and dislikes, hot
buttons to avoid and buttons to press, and general information
on what to do when such and such occurs. Such a manual
doesn't exist unless you write it. You are best acquainted with
you, your parent, and your stepparent. So you are left to on-the-
job training to become an expert in your relationships—what
works and what doesn't. However, this book offers general
behavior guidelines to spur your thinking and to help you shape
your relationship with Mom or Dad and your stepparent.

Use this book to spawn ideas of your own to be proactive
rather than reactive in your relationships. Rita Mae Brown

said, "A life of reaction is a life of slavery, intellectually and spiritually. One must fight for a life of action, not reaction." On occasion, people react in ways unbefitting an adult. Perhaps you recall a time when you did. If not, be grateful, because the result is regret for having said or done something inappropriate that offended someone else. Offensive behaviors are known to happen in stepfamilies and may become detrimental to the whole family. One way to prevent offense and emotional reactions is to have a good defense, or in other words, determine in advance what you will do to subdue emotional reactions to conscientious behavior and then practice it.

Love affects everyone, young and old, basically the same, causing us to say and do foolish things at times. Most of the time any offense is unintentional. Involuntary emotional and physical reactions are a good indication of how a perceived offense affects you. Your body may stiffen when embraced by your stepparent, or your response to an expression of endearment may be uncomfortably delayed. You also may unintentionally say foolish things to your stepparent without thinking of the consequences of misconstrued interpretation, causing misunderstanding. One offense leads to another, turning a minor problem into a major one. Most problems can be avoided if you think clearly and make a conscious decision about how to act.

Emotional reactions are natural, and often feel like a reflex. Feelings are not facts that are right or wrong, but rather are natural consequences of experiences. Even though you have little control over your feelings, unlike a reflex you can control your reaction and thus your behavior. Controlling your actions paints your desired masterpiece of your life and relationships.

Kristen experienced awkward situations, perhaps similar to yours, before and after her dad remarried. Kristen's training as a psychologist helped her to handle her emotions and potentially offensive behavior in a positive way. Kristen shared with me her method of avoiding offense and controlling her reactions: "Don't take things personally. Don't make assumptions—that's really crucial. We make assumptions like crazy. When somebody does something, we're sure it's about us. We don't always think about what we say, and we say things that are hurtful. That causes people to back away. Your parent's remarriage is about how relationships evolve. I have watched how the relationship between my dad and Mary and the whole family has evolved." Taking simple gestures personally often causes hurtful feelings that may prevent you from seeing reality. Emotional pain precludes growth of your developing friendship, thereby producing a negative evolution and a somber piece of art. Allow your stepparent time to get to know you and your family without judging his or her behavior as an affront to you.

Kristen described her initial reaction to a potentially offensive behavior, how she processed it, and her reaction to it: "When my stepmother redecorated my dad's condo and took down photos of my children when they were little and drawings they'd done, she gave them to me and asked if I wanted them. I felt like my whole family was being dismissed from my dad's life. I tried not to take it personally and to understand Mary's perspective. I would have gotten the photos and drawings eventually, and I know my dad doesn't care about things like that." Upon reflection Kristen realized Mary's action is common for women moving into their husband's home. Kristen knew her father wasn't particular about displaying grandchildren's photos. Rather than discarding pictures and drawings of sentimental value, Mary wanted to give them to the correct family. Kristen understood her stepmother's behavior was not being exclusionary but considerate. As she has experienced the growth of a cherished friendship, Kristen said, "It truly has been an evolvement." Kristen's ability to not take it personally allowed her to protect their emerging relationship.

Taking behavior personally may lead to false assumptions and interpersonal problems. Considering the offensive act rationally helps you to understand the behavior objectively. Potentially offensive behaviors are rarely meant to slight you but may in fact be an effort to reach out to you.

Kristen continued, "Acting rather than reacting is learning how to be objective. I would suggest to others to stand back and consider what's going on. Stand back and talk yourself through the situation. It's difficult when you are a part of it, but you can do it. I thought a lot about things before saying them, like what impact they might have. I also feel like I had my mother by my ear saying, 'Now Kristen, I want you to look at how this should be handled and you need to be open to this new relationship.'"

In order to be objective, remove yourself emotionally from the situation and try to view it from another's perspective. The same situation always looks different when it is happening to someone else. Looking at the situation from a different vantage point allows you to consider consequences of various reactions. For example, seeing the cause and solutions of a friend's problems and giving advice is easier than seeing the cause and solutions of personal problems. Like others, you may be better at giving advice than receiving it. Give yourself sound counsel then apply it in your interactions.

The third effort Kristen made was to think through different scenarios. Consider various consequences of emotional responses before acting. Then consider alternative behaviors. Knowing the possible consequences helps you to determine the most appropriate plan of action to develop loving relationships. Decide how to handle the situation to effectuate the relationship you desire. Rather than being vindictive, decide what you can do to enhance your friendship with your stepparent and support the new marriage. Kristen's wise counsel helps avoid undesirable behavior and hurtful consequences from emotional reactions. Your relationship with your parent and stepparent, your work of art in progress, reveals itself through your willingness to take action. Act now.

Be proactive in your interactions. Sometimes things are said or done that inadvertently annoy you. First, avoid taking your stepparent's actions personally and making false assumptions. Second, be objective by viewing the situation from someone else's perspective. Third, consider consequences of various options. Choose the consequences by choosing your actions. In this way you act rather than react to situations.

The Heart of the Matter

Your masterpiece emerges through your day-to-day interactions. With love as the medium in mixing and blending kindness, understanding, and compassion, your masterpiece becomes apparent. Just as the master artist projects feelings into her work of art, you project feelings into your relationships. The observer in tune with the artist feels what the artist wants felt. Likewise, family members in tune with you experience feelings you're projecting through your verbal and nonverbal behavior—strength, stamina, love, bitterness, anger, tenderness. Determine what you want to portray, then act accordingly. Circumstances are a product of behavior. If you are dissatisfied with your circumstances and want to paint a different relationship, then change your behavior. Harmonious relationships, like a true masterpiece, develop gradually. Expertise in this process is usually learned through trial and error and observation of master relationship artists.

The essence of this book is to empower you and me to become whom we desire to be and to develop the relationships we desire as much as is in our power. Families provide a true learning laboratory to practice the traits we wish to integrate into our personality. You cannot control the behavior of your parent or stepparent, but you can control your own, and thus paint the masterpiece of your dreams.

Resources

Bittman, Barry, "Laugh in the Face of Adversity: I'm Not Kidding," *www.touchstarpro.com*, 1998, 1999.

Brothers, Joyce, "Let Romance Keep You Young," *Parade*, 19 March 2006, p. 16.

Brown, Susan L., Jennifer Roebuck Bulanda, and Gary R. Lee, "The Significance of Nonmarital Cohabitation: Marital Status and Mental Health Benefits Among Middle-Aged and Older Adults," *Journal of Gerontology*, January 2005, 60B, 1, pp. S21–9.

Bulcroft, Richard A., and Kris A. Bulcroft, "The Nature and Functions of Dating in Later Life," *Research on Aging*, V. 13, No. 2, June 1991, pp. 244–60.

Carr, Deborah, "The Desire to Date and Remarry Among Older Widows and Widowers," *Journal of Marriage and Family*, November 2004, V. 66, Iss. 4, pp. 1051–68.

Carroll, Jason S., "Seeing Beyond the Wedding," *BYU Magazine*, Fall 2003, p. 55.

Child Development Institute, LLC, *childdevelopmentinfo.com*, "Stages of Social-Emotional Development in Children and Teenagers."

Corrie, Sarah, "Working Therapeutically with Adult Stepchildren: Identifying the Needs of a Neglected Client

Group," *Journal of Divorce & Remarriage,* V. 37 (½), 2002, pp. 135–50.

Court, Paula, "Holiday Traditions: Our Children Need Them Now," 21 December 2001, *www.nymetroparents .com/newarticle.cfm?colid=6804.*

Doherty, William J., "Divided Loyalties: The Challenge of Stepfamily Life," *Family Therapy Networker,* May/June 1999, pp. 32–38.

Eisenberger, Naomi I., M. D. Lieberman, and K. D. Williams, "Does Rejection Hurt? An fMRI Study of Social Exclusion," *Science,* 10 October 2003, V. 302, Iss. 5643, 290–92.

Ferber, Dan, "The Funny Factor: Why Smart Brains Take Humor Seriously," *Reader's Digest,* September 2006, pp. 100–5.

Gottman, John M., and Nan Silver, *Why Marriages Succeed or Fail* (New York: Fireside, 1994), pp. 29-57.

Grama, Joanna Lyn, "The 'New' Newlyweds: Marriage Among the Elderly, Suggestions to the Elder Law Practitioner," *Elder Law Journal,* 2000, V. 7, No. 2, pp. 379–407.

Gray, John, *Men Are from Mars, Women Are from Venus* (New York: HarperCollins, 1993), p. 30.

Larson, Jan, "Understanding Stepfamilies," *American Demographics*, July 1992, V. 14, Iss. 7, p. 360.

Marano, Hara Estroff, "Making Peace at Home: Remarried Couples Find New-Found Love, but Adult Children Aren't Always Happy," *Psychology Today*, 28 April 2004.

Moore, Thomas, *Original Self: Living with Paradox and Authenticity* (NY: HarperCollins, 2000), p. 25.

Moorman, Sara M., Alan Booth, and Karen L. Fingerman, "Women's Romantic Relationships After Widowhood," *Journal of Family Issues*, V. 27, No. 9, September 2006, pp. 1281–1304.

Orbuch, Terri L., Arland Thornton, and Jennifer Cancio, "The Impact of Marital Quality, Divorce, and Remarriage on the Relationships Between Parents and Their Children," *Marriage & Family Review*, 30 June 2000, V. 29, Iss. 4, p. 221.

Repplier, Agnes, *In Pursuit of Laughter* (Boston: Houghton Mifflin, 1936).

Roddick, Anita, *A Revolution in Kindness* (Anita Roddick Books, 2003).

Rutter, Virginia, "Lessons from Stepfamilies," *Psychology Today*, May/June 1994, Document ID: 1495.

Satir, Viginia, *The New Peoplemaking* (Mountain View, CA: Science and Behavior Books, 1988).

Smith, Ken R., Cathleen D. Zick, and Greg J. Duncan, "Remarriage Patterns Among Recent Widows and Widowers," *Demography*, V. 28, No. 3, August 1991, pp. 361–74.

Waite, Linda, and Maggie Gallagher, *The Case for Marriage: Why Married People Are Happier, Healthier, and Better Off Financially* (New York: Random House, 2001).

Index

About the Authors

Terri P. Smith graduated with a B.A. degree in communications from Brigham Young University. She met her husband, Paul, while working for the U.S. Senate in Washington, D.C. Terri has devoted the past twenty years to raising their four living children. In 2002, she began interviewing adult children and remarried, older couples to learn how they developed cherished friendships with mature stepfamily members. Terri shares the wisdom she gained from these interviews in *When Your Parent Remarries Late in Life*. To continue learning from you and others, she launched a Web site dedicated to adult stepchildren. Please visit her site at *www.graciousfamilylife.com* and feel free to share your story. She lives in West Orem, Utah.

James M. Harper, Ph.D. is the Director of the School of Family Life at Brigham Young University. He is a licensed psychologist and marriage and family therapist. He holds the highest honorary distinction given by the American Association for Marriage and Family Therapy, that of Fellow. Dr. Harper and his wife, Colleen, have five children.